The Arts of Cinema

The Arts of Cinema

Martin Seel

Translated by Kizer S. Walker

Cornell University Press
Ithaca and London

Originally published as: "Die Künste des Kinos"
© S. Fischer Verlag GmbH, Frankfurt am Main 2013.

The translation of this work was funded by Geisteswissenschaften
International—Translation Funding for Humanities and Social Sciences
from Germany, a joint initiative of the Fritz Thyssen Foundation, the
German Federal Foreign Office, the collecting society VG WORT and the
German Publishers & Booksellers Association.

First published 2018 by Cornell University Press

Printed in the United States of America

Library of Congress Cataloging-in-Publication Data

Names: Seel, Martin, author. I Walker, Kizer Sessoms, translator. I
    Translation of: Seel, Martin. Kunste des Kinos.
Title: The arts of cinema / Martin Seel ; translated by Kizer S. Walker.
Other titles: Kunste des Kinos. English Description: Ithaca : Cornell
    University Press, 2018. I Includes bibliographical references and index.
Identifiers: LCCN 2018001957 (print) I LCCN 2018002560 (ebook) I
    ISBN 9781501724855 (epub/mobi) I ISBN 9781501724862 (pdf) I
    ISBN 9781501709913 I ISBN 9781501709913 (cloth : alk. paper) I
    ISBN 9781501726170 (pbk. : alk. paper)
Subjects: LCSH: Motion pictures—Aesthetics. I Motion pictures—
    Philosophy. I Motion pictures and the arts.
Classification: LCC PN1995 (ebook) I LCC PN1995 .S4113 2018 (print) I
    DDC 791.4301—dc23
LC record available at https://lccn.loc.gov/2018001957

CONTENTS

THE ARTS OF CINEMA

OPENING CREDITS

Affairs

The arts of cinema issue from an affair with many other arts—with the high-wire acts of the rest of the art world, but with dramas of human emotion, thought, and action as well. Within a space of its own, cinema plays with the spaces and temporalities of the human world—with the light and shadow of that world, its noise and its silence, its narrowness and its expanse, its movement and its stasis. Cinema lets its audience be absently present.

Cinema's affairs are thus always affairs with us, with those who go to the movies now and then to be touched by films, and sometimes to let themselves be seduced. Cinema takes us along into a form of being in which we are allowed to relish its fluctuations utterly.

This state of being-moved that cinema, at its best, can induce in us takes its power from the relationships that film maintains with the other arts, which, for their part, have been entering into liaisons—sometimes secret, sometimes out in the open—with cinema for as long as it has existed. From the beginning, cinema has taken on various techniques from architecture, music, the stage, literature, and the visual arts; but it does not leave them unaltered. Cinema can do what it does because it reverses and transforms what the other arts can do.

These arts of cinema are the topic of this book. Art arises and evolves only in dialogue with other arts. As one among them, film participates in this conversation, communicating with the dreams and nightmares that sustain us throughout our lives.

The Site of the Cinema

The cinema is a designated site for the presentation of films. It is a social arena, created for the specific practice of interacting with films. It is by no means the only site of interaction with filmic images, however. Cinematic films—and certainly the many other types of film products—can be presented and experienced at many other sites as well: on television, on the computer screen, in museums, in the theater, in public viewing spaces, on the advertising surfaces in city squares. Today, many films can be picked up and played almost anywhere on mobile devices. Films and filmic images are almost everywhere. Only a few of these are made for the cinema, and only a few find their way to the cinema. Most forms of filmic images have long led a life that is independent of this arena. A book about the arts of cinema is thus not a book about "film" or "the medium" of film. Its sole subject is a primal scene of films' appearing.

Seen historically, film was born before the cinema and may, quite possibly, long outlive it. And yet a consideration of the cinema has a simple message to convey for every type of reflection on film: not much can be understood about the rest of the situations in which film is put to use without an understanding of the classical site of film's perception. In the theory of film, there is no way around the cinema.

"Film"

Another qualification must be mentioned here. This book is concerned with the most prominent variety of cinematic film, the feature film. With occasional side glances at other genres, I wish to consider what feature films, under the conditions of their presentation in the cinema, can do. When I speak of "films" in these pages without any modifier, this is what is intended. Of course, the focus on this specific case of the presence of films by no means rules out that filmic images can achieve some of what they can do in the cinema at other sites as well. I will leave this question open, however. This book is about the aesthetic potential of feature films as it is able to unfold first and foremost in the cinema.

This potential lies in the elementary forms of filmic presentation. Each film realizes this in its own way. What films present to their audiences consists in the possibilities they make available for their perception. Thus the composition of a film can only be determined together with the possibilities that it opens up for its own comprehension. Accordingly, the aesthetic potential of *film* consists in how particular films could potentially be experienced. These properties of film did not just fall from the sky, however. They are not simply built in to the techniques for the production of filmic images; rather, they have developed in the process of the production and the perception of films. And they continue to evolve. In that sense, an essay on film form contains a wager on what in the history of cinema will prove to be the most essential of its attractions.

Of course, the arsenals of cinema, just like those of the other arts, have been and still can be used to manipulative and ideological ends. For a long time, those who disdain cinema saw only this side of it and thus failed to recognize its artistic energies. This will be the sole focus of the present book, however: how feature films are able to realize their aesthetic potential in an artistic manner.

I investigate this disposition of film in a series of comparative reflections. The "film *as*" in the chapter titles, which places film in an intimate relationship with other arts and assets, should not be taken all too seriously. I am concerned here not with equivalences, but with differences. The point is to see what difference the cinema makes in the ensemble of human arts.

The Course of Things

My explorations begin with a survey of the fundamental elements of the cinematic film. Chapter 1 presents the particular spatiality of the filmic image in association with its acoustic dimension. Chapter 2 interprets film as a form of visual music, bringing to light the particular temporality of its trajectories. Chapter 3 elaborates on these observations by probing the ways in which the moving image differs from other types of image.

I expand upon these initial analyses and introduce a more nuanced treatment in the second third of the book. Chapter 4 is devoted to the particular visual attraction of film in its relationship to the performing arts. Chapter 5 examines the narrative disposition of cinema in its relationship to other storytelling practices. In a comparison of the fictional feature film and the documentary, chapter 6 discusses the relationship of film and reality. Films, we find, proceed in an explorative mode even where, in their fictions, they forgo realistic performance.

The last three chapters offer a further explication of the preceding phenomenology. Chapter 7 rejects illusionistic interpretations of the art of cinema and other arts, countering with a defense of film's imaginative constitution. Chapter 8 builds on this contention, proposing an alternative theory of the emotional power of cinema. Chapter 9 turns to film's internal affair with philosophizing. That chapter ends as the first one began: with a recollection of the artistic landscapes of individual films, the exploration of which can never be replaced with philosophical excursions.

The Film Program

In my reflections, I wish to conjoin two modes of thinking about film: my analysis of the arts of cinema will remain in constant contact with examples of the ways in which particular films realize their room-for-play.[1] With the exception of the book's conclusion, each chapter begins with the description of a film sequence that is suitable for illuminating the dimension that is under discussion. Each chapter ends with a sequence that further elucidates its theme. Along the way, many other films from diverse genres and periods come under discussion that shed their own light on the scenes of this book.

From this process emerges the book's film program. The main films, which I present in their own sections and occasionally revisit, include *The Searchers* by John Ford, *North by Northwest* by Alfred Hitchcock, *The Bourne Supremacy* and *United 93* by Paul Greengrass, *Zabriskie Point* and *Blow-Up* by Michelangelo Antonioni, *Perpetuum Mobile* by Nicolás

Pereda, *A Night at the Opera* by Sam Wood and the Marx Brothers, *Fontane Effi Briest* by Rainer Werner Fassbinder, *In the Mood for Love* by Wong Kar-Wai, *Goodfellas* by Martin Scorsese, *Apocalypse Now* by Francis Ford Coppola, and *Caché* by Michael Haneke.

The selection of these and the other films that are discussed or mentioned here follows neither a historical nor a hierarchical logic. The films are not intended to represent moments of transition in the history of cinema or any ranking of its greatest directors. In fact, they are not supposed to represent anything; they are intended to present something. The subject of this book is neither the tributaries of film history nor the branching history of film theory. Its subject is the appearing of films in the cinema. The film segments cited here stand for this.

One point of the selection is to foreground the heterogeneity of film production. From the auteur film to the blockbuster, multiple varieties of film will make their appearance. In the cinema, they all have their place. To attach a theory of cinema's arts to fetishized categories like "art film" or "filmic art" would be to misapprehend the theory's object. Popular cinema (relatively speaking) and elite cinema (relatively speaking) belong together. There are strong and weak films in both categories; for both, the strong ones can best demonstrate what films of the respective type can accomplish. Just as the techniques of cinema draw on the other arts precisely where they make no explicit reference to them, major and minor productions are in communication even—and in fact precisely—where they want nothing to do with each other.

Cinema is only one of the options for encountering the world and oneself in relation to art. All the arts are capable of introducing an audience to itself in a particular way. More radically than other types of art, films bring us close to that by which we wish to be determined. However much presence of mind, awareness, and understanding, however much pleasure in interpretation or art of interpretation that individual films might demand of their audience, the cinema remains above all a place to indulge in involuntary receptivity. In the cinema we celebrate the passive side of our existence, without the enjoyment of which all of our activities would be to some degree futile. The ethos of cinema consists in the challenge to let things be. It is not tied to any more far-reaching demands. All that the arts of cinema expect of us is that we be moved by their movement of light and dark.

1

FILM AS ARCHITECTURE

A Beginning

After the opening credits of John Ford's film *The Searchers* (USA, 1956), the screen goes black for a brief moment. A title fades in in white script: "Texas 1868." The screen goes black again. In the next moment, three things happen at once. The sound of a door latch is heard, the bittersweet musical leitmotif is introduced; a door swings open, revealing the silhouette of the woman who has just opened it, and, with that, the space of the film is opened.

This first shot establishes a stark contrast between the interior space, which fills out three-quarters of the screen and remains completely dark, and the sharply demarcated exterior space of a wide-open landscape bathed in bright light. This visual composition alludes to a fundamental conflict of this film (and countless other films, well beyond the Western genre): a vulnerable protective space finds itself at the mercy of a threatening space of action; an ominous outside yearns for a pacified interior; an oppressive inside longs for a liberating exterior. The subsequent tracking shot follows the woman in her path to the front porch of the house, gradually widening the image of the landscape. Here again the movement of the film is anticipated: in the vastness of the country lurks a threat to its social and legal domestication. In the right half of the image, a rider can be seen approaching from the distance, followed by the woman's nervous gaze. A man steps up next to her and, with a questioning intonation, utters the first word of the film, giving its hero a name: "Ethan?"

The film never explicitly answers the question of what is the matter with Ethan Edwards. Yet in these first thirty seconds of action, the door is opened for a view of the construction of a filmic world. It provides a glimpse not only of this film's architecture, but that of films in general. This opening gesture holds a clue to the relationship between architecture and film. Each in its own way is an art of spatial construction. And like all arts, both are also temporal arts: they present a maneuver to their viewers and users or demand a maneuver of them that would be impossible without the construction of an edifice or a film.

Division of Space

Architecture's fundamental operation lies in a process of dividing and organizing space. In the process, differences are established between inside and outside that can be repeated, modified, mirrored, and disrupted again and again. Every building gives rise to a space *of* spaces, separated from or open to each other in various ways. Many buildings not only establish a boundary between interior and exterior space; they bring about a replication of their space as well. At the same time, this ensemble of spaces forms a space *for* spaces by engendering linkages and passageways, parapets and thresholds, views out and views in, that relate to each other in various ways. They communicate not only inwardly, but outwardly as well: with buildings and trees, with light and shadow, with calm and noise, in short, with everything to which the building opens itself in the surroundings of its location. This shows us that every structure engenders a space *within* spaces. It places a plural space inside a larger space that is likewise a product of a diversity of forces. The places where the individual building realizes its effect are always geographical, cultural, historical, and quotidian places. These spaces where a structure stands, however, are ultimately always linked to *a particular* space: the space of a landscape that belongs to a building from the moment of its construction and to which, with its construction, it has lent its own accent.

As in the case of architectural spaces in the literal sense, the space through which filmic motion leads us is a constructed one through and through. No less than the space of architecture, it derives from operations of spatial division and spatial organization—and of the replication, opening up, and closing off of spaces as well. Like architecture, film generates a space *of* spaces and *for* spaces within the totality of a space that is incalculably vast. Thus every point in my outline of the dynamics of architectonic space applies as well to the space of movement that is characteristic of film. One of these spaces we can actually enter, however, bringing about continual shifts in perspective in relation to the movement of our bodies. In contrast, we are subjected to the movements of the other space within its own architectonic space—the cinema—with no influence whatsoever on the rhythm of its perspectives and its vistas. In the first case, we move within a space or in its vicinity; in the second, we are confronted with the autonomous motion of a visual space.

The parallels between architecture and film can thus only be illuminating if we are able to identify the decisive difference, beyond the obvious ones, between filmic and architectonic space. The salient point lies in the divergent operations for dividing space. The basic distinction between interior and exterior space in architecture corresponds to that between *on screen* and *off screen* in film. The movement of film proceeds as a constant interchange between that which appears on the screen and that which is not yet, no longer, or not at all visible on it (it is even active, as potential interchange, in the case of extreme static shots). The interior/exterior relationships that become visible *in* film—views out and views in, movement of the camera's gaze, fade-ins, fade-outs, panning shots, saccades, and so forth—are organized in the medium of a differential between what is visible on the screen at that moment and what is invisible. By means of the framing and montage of image segments, films establish the specific space of their action: the space *within which* everything that occurs in films occurs, and at the same time a space *which itself* occurs as the filmic events unfold.

Ambient Sound

Ever since films in the cinema have been accompanied by music, and particularly since the advent of the sound film, the acoustic dimension has played an essential role in the filmic construction of space. Through music, speech, and other sounds, what is visible as well as what is invisible on the screen is accentuated and sculpted in various ways. Depending on how sound sources are localized with respect to the scenes appearing on the screen, acoustic effects establish complex interior/exterior relations that correspond in a number of ways to the visual organization of space. The sources of sound may be contained within the scene that is visible on the screen or located outside of it. Sounds that characterize a scene from the outside may likewise be located within the situations produced by the film or—as in the case of "film music" or forms of the voice-over—they may be deployed without such localization. These basic options for the acoustic organization of films may be held more or less distinct one from the other or they may run together fluidly. They may be combined within a single scene or over the course of a film. However sound is deployed, films' acoustic sphere is always a dimension of the event space, which is opened up by means of these processes. From an aesthetic standpoint, one of the primary functions of the soundtrack is to broaden and enrich the filmic space of spaces—not only as an elaboration of what is taking place on the screen at any particular moment, but also by forging an interconnection of filmic space with the space that is presented in the film. In the cinema, the sound space becomes ambient sound.

Every type of building possesses a particular acoustics. Ideally, considerable attention is devoted to acoustics in the construction of concert and lecture halls, churches and cinemas. As resonance spaces for complex acoustic events, these structures are themselves sound chambers within which the effect of particular acoustic events can unfold in the most appropriate way possible. It was not without basis that Hegel, in his *Lectures on Aesthetics*, attributed an "architectonic character" to music, which he characterized as a "building of sound." Paul Valéry is following the same trace in his dialogue "Eupalinos, or the Architect," when he emphasizes music's magic of forming and transforming spaces.[1] This affinity between architectonic space and musical time sheds light on the particular architectures of film. Its acoustic motion allows the movement of the film image to intervene in the space of its perception. The sound of films fills the space of their appearing in an altogether literal sense: sound surrounds the audience and only in so doing draws it into the film's visual landscape. In this way, the composition of acoustic events links the virtual space of films with the real space of their presentation, the space occupied by bodies. This is accomplished by means of sound sources that maintain an intimate relationship to everything that takes place on the screen.

Some Opening Credits

The click of a door latch, a musical leitmotif, the first words of dialogue—the opening of the *plot* of the film *The Searchers* strikes a three-note chord. A sound is audible, music sets a mood, verbal comments are made about an initial event as the audience is brought into the setting of the film. The opening of the *film*, on the other hand, does not give any insight into its space of action. Its opening credits run for a minute and a half. First the Warner Brothers seal and then the name of the producer appear against a plain background image (a conventionally painted brick wall). Next, the actor portraying Ethan Edwards is named in black print: John Wayne. Only then is the film's title faded-in in bright red script. These initial twenty-three seconds are accompanied by dramatic orchestral music, which fades out and is replaced by Stan Jones's sentimental Western song "The Searchers," while the rest of the credits roll. The song dies away while the screen goes black twice; it is immediately followed by the film's theme melody as the door to the fictional space is opened.

Even for the standards of the time, these are decidedly austere opening credits. They present a stark contrast to the artful opening of the film story. The three different musical themes, which will make their appearances again later in the film, foreshadow the unstable mood of the plot as it will develop. They fill the space of the cinema even before the visible space of the film has opened up. At the outset, everything remains visually flat. Before the narrative action begins, the acoustic events swing into action. The landscape of the film is there before its landscape is revealed. It enfolds the spectators even before they find themselves in it by sight.

Landscapes

Sound and resonance are the pillars of film architecture.[2] Their function is to divide and connect spaces, to shift spaces and nest one within the next, to survey and conceal and in this way to generate a space of spaces and for spaces. This is, however, a space in which each of the respective visible spaces remains open to the intangible sphere of the world presented by the film. This status of filmic space is responsible for the landscape character of films' presence. The experience of landscape essentially arises from a position amid a heterogeneous and variable profusion of conditions and events that always exceed its subjects' capacity to take in and understand. Landscape experienced aesthetically has the character of a space that is occurring. With respect to buildings, this amounts to the presence of the breadth of the real world within which the edifice occupies a position and with regard to which it takes a position. In cinema, this effect arises from the fact that a film never offers its audience anything approaching a complete image of the space in which its story plays out, but only aspects of the same, which must be supplemented in a game of memory and anticipation, without ever coming together as a comprehensible whole. In the montage of visual and acoustic events, films produce a space in motion that also moves the audience, a space that is experienced as a *fragment* of the filmic world.

Filmic events possess this character independently of whether or the extent to which natural or urban landscapes play a role in them. Even in a film like *The Man Who Shot Liberty Valance* (John Ford, USA, 1962), which is concerned throughout with the right of land appropriation and the cultivation of the landscape, these processes are largely excluded from the visuals, apart from short sequences at the beginning and end. Instead, the concept of landscape character formally determines the type of spatial movement that characterizes the appearing of films in the cinema. Their architecture affords the possibility of establishing for their viewers a position within and amid a scene and sequence of events that are explored in the course of the film, producing constantly shifting relationships of interior and exterior, visible and invisible, familiar and uncanny, present and absent. In this way, the spectators can enter perceptually into a space that is beyond their bodily grasp and allow themselves to be animated, in their seeing and hearing, their feeling and understanding, by what happens *in that space* and how *that space itself* happens. The filmic division of space does not organize, accentuate, duplicate, and change an already-existing space, but rather produces—no less than literal architecture does, yet differently—an experience of space sui generis.

This is the source of a fundamental priority of the space of movement over the space of meaning. The settings in which film performances take place derive from films' spatial movement. Anything that they might want to "say" to us, that they show us by documentary or fictitious means (or both), depends on the spaces through which they guide us—on spaces that are shown to us in such a way that they are always, at the same time, concealed from our gaze. This is how filmic architecture operates: it builds a world in which we are allowed to sojourn in our perception, without really being in it. This virtuality of filmic space, however, is extremely real. It is dependent on the appearing of a visual and sonic movement, which ensnares viewers in processes of a sensate apprehending[3] that are thoroughly bound up with the improbable existence of this appearing.

Two Extremes

One of the most ingenious examples of filmic architecture is achieved in an almost completely empty space—in the famous cornfield scene, filmed near Bakersfield, California, in Alfred Hitchcock's *North by Northwest* (USA, 1959). In this case, the landscape *in* the film serves as an object lesson in the formation of the landscape *of* a film. Roger O. Thornhill (Cary Grant), a supposed CIA agent, is sent by the beautiful double agent, Eve Kendall (Eva Marie Saint) into the clutches of spies who are out for his life. Having arrived at the appointed place, Thornhill stands alone in an open field and—in an editing sequence that begins with extreme calm and becomes increasingly frenetic—awaits his fate, which he ultimately escapes with a bang.

This nearly ten-minute sequence begins with a dissolve from a close-up of Kendall's face to a long shot of an expanse of harvested cornfields bisected by a straight road. The last strains of music from the previous scene fade away. The action that follows forgoes music. From a static point of view we see the intercity bus approach and Thornhill get off in the middle of nowhere. The bus leaves the scene at the lower right edge of the screen.

It can still be heard long after it is out of sight. This is followed by a calm alternation between objective and subjective shots that show the searching glances of the elegantly dressed New York adman as he stands there perplexed. The few vehicles that speed past on the dusty road only serve to underscore the emptiness of the farmland. Soon the crop duster that will attack Thornhill can be heard in the background, and then it comes into view. Initially, it functions as yet another spatial indicator marking the boundlessness of the scene. Then, with a distinct and steady rhythm, visible space contracts more and more tightly around the central figure as the would-be assassins close in from above. The space and time of the episode are artificially stretched, only to be concentrated, ultimately, at a single point.

Part of the irony of the scene lies in the fact that, in a terrain that appears to offer no protection to the beleaguered hero, two spaces of escape are still to be found. The first is a not-yet-harvested cornfield, which enters our field of vision in passing early in the scene, and there Thornhill seeks cover. The attacking plane drives him out with a dusting of pesticide. Coughing and wheezing, he looks for a way out. Through a window framed left and right by cornstalks, Thornhill can see a tanker truck approaching on the road; the suffocating interior space allows a view into the open. Thornhill saves himself by forcing the truck to a stop at the last moment. Close-up of the hood of the approaching truck; honking and the sound of screeching brakes. Cut. Close-up of Thornhill's panicked face; honking, screeching brakes. Cut. Close-up of the hood; honking, brakes. Cut. Medium close-up: Thornhill lets himself fall beneath the driver's cab; screeching brakes. Cut. Medium close-up: Thornhill lies under the truck; engine sound. The space has narrowed to the smallest possible scope. The vastness of the landscape has now disappeared entirely. Cut. Medium close-up: Thornhill looks in the direction of the approaching biplane; engine sound. Cut. Shot widens: the swaying airplane steers toward the truck; engine noise. Cut. Long shot: road, fields; the airplane crashes into the rear of the truck's tank; explosion; dramatic music starts. The music marks the beginning of the end of the episode and the resolution of its tension. During the final shot, the filmic space gradually opens up again in a comic ending.

Vincenzo Natali's film *Cube* (Canada, 1997) presents a converse case of spatial construction. Various characters, who will gradually come together as a group, inexplicably—to both the characters and the film's audience—find themselves in a gigantic enclosure consisting of colored cubes illuminated by an indirect light. Cryptic ornaments that look like technical drawings can be seen on the walls of the cubes. The film leads its characters and viewers through this maze made up of—as we learn—17,577 cubes circulating within one giant cube, some of which are outfitted with deadly traps. These spaces within a space open to each other, only to automatically close up again. The entire film plays out in this situation, in which, with the exception of the final shot, there is no outside, and thus no protective inside. Apart from the one that is reached at the end of the story line, no cube leads to a space outside of the shell that encases everything. And even that one comes into appearance only as a dazzling brightness into which the only surviving character disappears; nothing is visible within it. The audience is engaged with configurations of space and time that extend much further than those traversed in the course of the film.

These extremes of a nearly completely open and a nearly completely closed space demonstrate that neither filmic nor architectonic space can be conceived and produced without reference to an exterior space and thus to a framework of interior and exterior spaces. Like architecture, film is a process of and between spaces. In this respect it is always the *event* of a space that is opened up by means of buildings and furnished with a dynamized imagination by means of films. An anthropological constant makes itself equally felt in literal and in filmic architectonics. In a pure interior, we risk suffocation; in a pure exterior, we risk getting lost. In either situation we long for the opposite. The landscapes of cinema present this antagonistic and thus labile desire again and again. Yet as much as the cinema plays with this double desire—now cheerfully, now gloomily, now brutally, now soothingly, and not infrequently in all of these modes at once—it also plays with its double satisfaction. For cinema always keeps open an interior in the exterior, and an exterior in the interior.

An Ending

The final scene of John Ford's *The Searchers* also dramatizes this openness of filmic space. As the Western song is heard for a second time (immediately following a change of mood produced, in part, by the film's

musical leitmotif), the camera pulls back into the interior of the farmhouse, leaving the restless Ethan Edwards to an uncertain fate in the vastness of the prairie. This closing shot reproduces the opening one, which
has already been repeated once in the middle of the film, but now in
the reverse direction. With this second repetition at the end of the film,
Ethan, after the long years of searching, returns Debbie (Natalie Wood),
who had been kidnapped by Indians, to the neighbors of her murdered
parents. Mr. and Mrs. Jorgensen (John Qualen and Olive Carey) receive
the young woman with compassion, leading her into the house, toward
the camera that moves backward into the house's interior. Once again, the
cutout of the door and the view of the bright landscape it reveals fill
barely a third of the screen; as in the first scene, they are framed by the
black of the interior walls. Ethan Edwards takes a few steps in the direction of the house door, then turns to let Martin Pawley (Jeffrey Hunter)
and Laurie Jorgensen (Vera Miles), the reunited young couple, go past; he
turns toward the house again, hesitates, turns around, and strides slowly
away. At that moment, the door of the house swings shut. Yet *no one*, no
figure *in* the house, closes it. All of the characters have exited to the right,
but the door closes from the left. No sound of the latch is to be heard.
At the same time, the sentimental song is replaced by the chords of the
stirring orchestral music with which the film's opening credits began (although now the sequence of the melodies is reversed). With the closing of
the door, the space of the film also closes of its own accord. Nearness and
distance, outside and inside, all fade to black. There is no more division
of space, only a black pictorial ground with the insert "The End." The
screen becomes a wall again, demarcating the space of the cinema; it no
longer functions as a passage to a space in motion within that space. As is
often the case in art, such self-presentation of the artistic medium serves
to further intensify what that medium presents in its particular utiliza-
tion. Here the closing of the space of fiction is at the same time an expul-
sion of the hero from the world that that fiction projects. In the context
of a community preoccupied with the project of civilization, there is no
room for a character in whom nearly superhuman qualities are coupled
with inhuman ones. The allegory of the filmic image converges with the
allegory of the social dislocation of the modern hero.

This passage is not only emblematic of a divided desire simultaneously
for the safe harbor of the interior and the liberation of the exterior, which

drives the narrative in many films. It demonstrates as well an essential excerpt character of film space, which is evident precisely in shots that offer a view into a vast, open space. Every relationship established with situations and events, this scene makes clear, is accompanied in film by a permanent withdrawal; all that is visible of the filmic events produces a horizon line demarcating that which remains invisible in these events and exerting a palpable effect on everything that is manifest within the image. Together with its opening, the end of *The Searchers* can be interpreted as a staging of the unstable framing that, at least potentially, underlies all filmic events.

Spatial Imagination

The formation of space in film is always characterized by this variable perimeter. It allows us to see that filmic space is incomparably more open *and* more closed, at once more stable *and* more unstable, than any space in which we might otherwise find ourselves and move about. Filmic space is more closed and more stable because the movement to which this space is subject and which takes place within this space occurs independently of the position of the perceiver, in an unalterable sequence. Everything about this motion is predetermined; every spectator is subject to it. Yet this space is more open and more unstable precisely because it is a space in motion that always follows the law of its own dynamics. The horizon within which appears whatever is to be seen does not shift or merge in relation to the bodily movement of the spectators; it holds them fast and veers around with them while constantly withdrawing. For while a horizon might be visible *within* the image, the horizon *of* the image is not visible. It lies outside of the image frame, but in a fundamentally different way than in the case of other pictorial forms. The space of films does not exceed *our* horizons—only the best manage to do that—it exceeds *its own* horizons. With each shot, each cut, each pan, each zoom, each object that is moved into or out of the visible field, the domain of everything that lies outside of its appearing changes, without this outside becoming present except in constantly shifting perspectives.[4]

That is why filmic space is an imagined space—not only because it is *generated* by imagination, not only because it must be *augmented* by the imagination of the audience, but because it moves, along with everything that is visible in it, within an invisible horizon. This makes the experience of filmic space one of being transported into a world that, in its accessibility, remains permanently inaccessible, a combination that occurs only in film. Filmic space is a mobile viewing space that sets the audience in a perceiving motion, one that points beyond itself precisely at the point where it allows itself to be bound by the play of visible appearances within it.

More Opening Credits

Many of these relations coalesce in a filmic aphorism such as the one conveyed in the opening credits of Hitchcock's *North by Northwest*. After the roar of the Metro-Goldwyn-Mayer lion, blue lines of an architectural drawing form on a green background, tracing the grid structure of the façade of a New York high-rise; the animation is accompanied by the dramatic music of Bernard Herrmann, which is also deployed at the end of the cornfield scene and in the film's finale. In a slow dissolve, the façade itself comes into view, together with the life of the city, mirrored in its windows, as well as a diminutive slice of the sidewalk in front of the building, which is visible in the lower right corner of the screen. A world is sketched out here that resembles the real one in many of its features and points of reference, yet it is a world in which a story will unfold that has never taken place in the real world. The glass façade of the high-rise building functions as a screen on the screen that places before the eyes of the audience—once again—the dialectics of spatial division that we have already addressed in this chapter. Whether in front of a building or inside it, or in the cave of the cinema, wherever we pursue an inward orientation, we orient ourselves outwardly at the same time. The spaces we pass through, whether bodily or only perceptually, keep us mindful of the ones that are absent, temporarily or permanently. While architectonic spaces are without a doubt considerably more stable than film's mercurial and fleeting spaces built of sound and image, both forms of construction—the one employing stone and steel no less than the one making use of light and shadow—lead us into spaces within the space of our lives, and we need their literal and metaphoric motion like we need air to breathe.

2

FILM AS MUSIC

A Prelude

Ten minutes into Michelangelo Antonioni's film *Zabriskie Point* (USA, 1970) there is a short transitional scene. A young man (Mark Frechette) and his roommate are driving through Los Angeles in a rusty pickup, heading to the campus of their university, which is marked by protests and police deployment. This passage, barely two minutes in length, has no major role in the film's plot. But formal forces are at work in it that drive the story's narrative to its spectacular end; it forms a prelude to everything that follows. The sequence begins with an inane advertising image of a steer on the side of a meat truck. The truck moves past the camera, revealing behind it a façade painted with a grotesque rustic scene that, for a moment, forms the background of the film scene. As these static images are left behind, an increasingly wild movement of images unfolds, surveying a chaotic urban landscape. The billboards and lettering that everywhere adorn the streets and vehicles already create a profusion of heterogeneous signals. At first, the trip is accompanied by realistic sounds, but twenty-three seconds into the segment, the shrill tones of electronic music set in, mixing nearly indistinguishably with the traffic noise of the city (the original music for the film is by Pink Floyd). This jungle of sound corresponds to a sudden opacity in the progression of images as a freight train clattering past is placed in the picture in a way that temporarily dissolves all definable figures in a sort of filmic action painting—a sharp contrast to the manicured, palm-lined boulevard that leads to the campus.

This trip leads through an event space that is as fragmented as it is saturated with forms. The structural violence that is the subject of the narrative is already at work here. A commercial district is presented as if it were an unleashed force of nature, its creations leading a life of their own, independent of the intentions of the users of the space. Yet at the same time the film's staging elicits a remarkable beauty from this wasteland of civilization and the ugliness of the terrain. The ossified relations of an industrial zone are transformed into a visual dance.

The progression of images that develops is a kind of music in its own right. Let us forget for a moment that sound and resonance play a key role in this sequence from *Zabriskie Point*. Let us switch off the audio for this and all other films and allow them to be silent for a moment. In this way, it becomes discernible just how tightly the imagination of filmic space is bound up with the imagination of filmic time. This is so much the case that it is possible to comprehend film's visual events not only as a form of architecture (though not a proper one, to be sure), but also as a form of music (though, again, not a proper one). It is because the visual energy of film is itself a musical energy that film has succeeded in connecting with the sphere of sound in the way that it has in the course of its history.

More than any other medium, it is music that has traditionally been known for its ability to both inspire and present, though its art, movement of the body and the spirit. Unlike architecture, music *is* movement; it performs movement and seduces its listeners with it. What connects music and architecture and at the same time separates them is an alternative mode of integrating spaces and times. Just as architecture operates with processes of spatial organization and in so doing also modifies the experience of *time* in its constructions, music operates with techniques of temporal organization, thereby also altering the experience of *space* within its audible range. In its way, cinema appropriates both operations. The appearing of filmic spaces is at the same time an appearing of lived and livable time.[1]

Time Connections

Music's basal process is the generation of rhythms and tonal relationships. All music works with intervals of times and tones—with caesuras within an acoustic event. It progresses as an unfolding of a constellation of audible events whose motion is frequently perceived as a literal or metaphorical expression of human motion and emotion. Yet regardless of the extent to which it possesses such expressive qualities, all music follows a process of *suspense:* the buildup, relief, and conversion of tensions within the experience of time. Music creates ordered time: a present shot through with memory and expectation that, over the course of the musical event, makes itself felt in a lasting transience. Making something of finite time: this is what music shows us.

The cinema audience has a similar experience. Something is always slipping away that is already irretrievable; something is always emerging that cannot yet be grasped. This visual rhythm is a formal privilege of the filmic image for which the still image has no equivalent. Films are music for the eye. Like music, film is a presentation in motion, which its audience often encounters as a presentation of emotion.

Only in a secondary sense is this due to the fact that film *is* always also music, accompanied from its early days by voice and music and later equipped with a soundtrack. Under the conditions of the sound film, the old silent films and their occasional, latter-day descendants are no longer mute; with regard to the absence of sound and voice, they operate with an acoustics of silence, as, for instance, in *Un chant d'amour* (Jean Genet, France, 1950) or *The Artist* (Michel Hazanavicius, France, 2011). In the first place, however, as Angela Keppler writes, it is "the dynamic of the images themselves that make film an analogue of the musical event." Keppler continues:

> It renews in a visual manner the paradox, known from music, of a performance from which one cannot escape because it is constantly escaping. Film

involves its spectators in a spatial event of which they have no overview; at the same, however, since it is realized by means of image movement, it involves them in an event in which they are *not* themselves involved. . . . It manages to bind *its* present to the performance of *a* present and to bind that, in turn, closely to *our* present. With a reality that is held at arm's length, it manages to cut close to the skin.[2]

In the here and now, the cinematic film invites us on a journey through time in shifting constellations of the *here* and *there*, as well as the *still*, the *not yet*, and the *no longer*.

Action (1)

Audiences' pleasure in action scenes is scarcely understandable apart from their receptivity to the metaphorical music that accompanies those sequences. Typically, there are many things happening at once in these scenes, but often nothing or nearly nothing happens that is of any consequence to the progress of the fictional plot. More often than not, one knows or at least suspects which of the characters—whether played by John Wayne or Cary Grant, Arnold Schwarzenegger or Bruce Willis, Jodie Foster or Uma Thurman—will come out of it, more or less battered, but alive. The main thing—and not infrequently the only thing—is *how*. In a climax of deliberate actions and chance occurrences, the cinema savors the possibilities of its visual choreography, sometimes to the point of excess. It takes a restless break from narrative—a time-out that sometimes constitutes the main point of the filmic spectacle.

Even for its time, the cornfield scene from *North by Northwest* considered in the previous chapter was an unusual action sequence in the ostentatiously slow pace of its development. Today's cinema has heightened the tempo of image montage and image movement considerably, and not only on technical grounds. Toward the end of the film *The Bourne Supremacy* by Paul Greengrass (USA, 2004), Jason Bourne (Matt Damon) finds himself pursued, yet again, by multiple tormentors. In Moscow, a hitman, his mafia backers, and the police are all on his heels. The whole episode lasts about nine minutes. After a prelude in which Bourne, beaten and then wounded by gunshot, is on foot, there is a furious car chase through the streets of the city that runs for five minutes.

Let us mute this film, too, for the time being, so that we may fully attend to its dynamic of visible movement alone. First of all, there is a play of colors. Bourne commandeers a yellow taxi, which immediately acquires its first dent and by the end of the chase will be reduced to scrap. The hitman pursues him in a black Mercedes SUV; it is backed up by black Mercedes sedans outfitted with blue rooftop lights. The police join the rally with modest blue and white cars with blue and red emergency lights. This power ratio not only makes evident that a man is on the run against all odds; the color markers create a visual chord, at the same time ensuring that the different parties are identifiable. Against views of the wintery gray city rushing past with its slick streets, traffic lights, crosswalks, stately buildings, onion domes, billboards, and ad banners—and in contrast to other vehicles on the streets—the three basic colors form a constantly shifting optical leitmotif in the overall choreography. The latter is dominated by a vortex of heterogeneous shots often lasting only fractions of a second. Low-angle and overhead shots, close-up, medium, and long shots, tracking shots and exaggerated pans, are presented in incessant fluctuation. The perspectives of the two protagonists from inside their vehicles shift rapidly to exterior views. In addition, many of the close-ups show the faces of Bourne and his pursuer, the movements of their gazes and their steering, fragments of their vehicles, and the surfaces and forms that rush past. The continual maneuvers of overtaking and evading create a martial ballet of actors that accelerate and brake, skid and spin, draw near and fall behind, collide and wedge together, or remain stranded behind on a stage space that is itself in constant motion.

The hectic revue ends in the chiaroscuro of a tunnel, shot through with the light of overhead lamps, in which the situation becomes even more opaque. In heavy traffic, Bourne has shaken off almost all of his pursuers, but the hitman's attacks are becoming more and more aggressive. Sparks fly as the taxi is forced against the wall of the tunnel; dense smoke rises as the assassin shoots his opponent's tires. Now the hitman loses his overview of the situation, which the audience has long since lost. His SUV crashes into a cement column. Pistol drawn, Bourne gets out of his car and assures himself that his pursuer is incapacitated. Against the headlights of the line of cars that has formed at the site of the crash, Bourne limps toward the tunnel exit. In this final shot of the episode, the hero is seen from the back in black silhouette against a dim wall. Pallid light falls into the image from above. It is not a radiant victor, but a beaten winner who leaves the scene, which a moment before had been the setting of the most violent of image movements. Laden with the burden of his dark past (which remains obscure for him and for the audience), he goes on his way alone.

Double Motion

"[T]he chief task of music," Hegel tells us, "consists in making resound, not the objective world itself, but, on the contrary, the manner in which the inmost self is moved to the depths of its personality and conscious soul."[3] The visual energy of film cannot be reduced to this conception of music and musicality, however, even though the representation of inner experience often plays a particularly prominent role in feature films. For the cinema can also entail the pure attraction of an elaborate "objective" movement, one that gives no expression to the stirring of subjective emotion (the segments from *Zabriskie Point* and *The Bourne Supremacy* are cases in point). Instead, this movement generates a dynamic in its own right, one that is capable of captivating by means of its rhythm alone. This rhythm is always a double one. The movements *in* the image are always intertwined with movements *of* the image. A film's music arises from the harmony of these processes. This opens up endless possibilities of visual composition. Camera movement and montage can operate congruously or incongruously vis-à-vis frenzied motion or stillness within the image, while these latter conditions, for their part, may remain stable or change according to various calculations. The shaping of the image movement forms the view of what happens on the screen; the events in the images form the shape in which they are presented. At both levels, a continual giving and taking, appearing and disappearing, persisting and elapsing, take place.

The definitive difference between acoustic music and the music of film images lies once again—as in our comparison of film and architecture—in a difference in their fundamental operations. If the former works with intervals of tempos and tones or sounds, which can only be followed by hearing, the latter works with intervals of tempos and visual appearing, which can only be followed by sight. Perception, in both cases, takes place within a tension of memory and expectation with respect to what is audible or visible in the moment; in both cases, it is subjected to a continual suspension of what is happening in the present moment. Despite these similarities, the disparate modes of sensorial appearing generate different ways of binding the audience to the artistic event. As long as the spectators do not shut their eyes or leave the room, they remain, in a double sense, oriented toward the visible progression of a film. Their perception is oriented toward what can be seen on the screen and, at the same time, toward how the particular film presents it to the eye. The capacity to focus the spectator's attention, via film, on *what is shown* is always based on control over *how it is shown*: on the composition of image sequences that allow what is shown to come into appearing in a particular *gestus*.

Thus not only in the unfolding of filmic space, but in that of filmic time as well, a fundamental primacy of movement before meaning holds sway. The latter arises from the former. Everything that a film presents is presented within a time that is organized through the operations of camera and montage. In everything that it presents, the film presents *its* time. The imagined space of a film is thus simultaneously imagined time and vice versa. Together they engender an imagination to which the spectators inevitably succumb, however actively they may exercise their own imaginations in the process.

This doubling of the image event and events in the image has no equivalent in pure music. Music presents *itself* to its listeners, as Hegel asserts, without *representing* anything. Here there is nothing like the interplay between movement within the image and movement of the image that defines the visual composition of filmic processes. And there are still other differences between the presentation and reception of musical pieces and filmic "music." In the cinema, a film presents precisely the same visual (and sonic) event at every screening. By contrast, each musical performance represents an individual variation (and interpretation) of its event, even when the same musicians play the same piece again and again—and this is not even to mention, for the moment, musical forms that by their improvisational nature never produce the same constellation of sounds twice. But even where, thanks to its conservation in storage media, exactly the same music plays again and again, a central distinction remains. In the cinema, because the audience is compelled to be present with seeing eyes, the narrative course of the film produces an intensified temporal dictate compared to the aural transport afforded by sonic processes. Unlike music in the literal sense, attention to a film demands of an audience that it face the proceedings in permanent bodily concentration. The visual rhythm of a film imposes a relentless process of caesura from which one can turn away only at the price of disengaging from the film's development.

Action (2)

Of course, we must also bear in mind that, in sound film, the configurations of image movement can be interpenetrated at any time by acoustic operations of all sorts. It is time, then, that we switch on the sound again and reconnect the metaphorical music of film with actual sound, which shares responsibility for the full dramaturgy of most film narratives. Sound in film is by no means only a matter of musical episodes, but consists as well of noises, voices, and other types of acoustical effects, mixed in various proportions to create the events that are audible in the cinema and that interact in a variety of ways with what is visible and invisible on the screen. It is only through this interaction that film becomes the audiovisual art that it has represented since the invention of the sound film.

The soundtrack of the chase scene in *The Bourne Supremacy* represents a veritable audio drama in its own right. Even only *hearing* the passage, it is easy to recognize what sort of action is taking place. Road noise is audible, in constant variation: howling engines, screeching tires, sirens, honking, the crash and clatter of collisions. Apart from the radio transmissions, in Russian, of the hitman and his accomplices, there are no voices to be heard. Where the Bakersfield scene in *North by Northwest* presented only a few acoustic spatial indicators, here we are confronted with a profusion of such signals. They model and accentuate the event space in multiple ways. They not only make audible what is unseen and augment the dimensions of the space of action; they also expand the filmic space itself. Honking, the din of sirens, engine noise, and so on keep speeding *past*. For one thing, this creates a perspective on the action from the point of view of the hunted protagonist, since it is primarily from his standpoint that these sounds are heard. It also puts the events in perspective for the spectators, who likewise experience them from the center of the action.

The series of scenes has an underscore of music (John Powell) marked by a driving beat, whose open nodal lines mix with the other sounds, now louder, now softer. This music is not located in the story world of the film. It is not a sign of simulated reality. Instead, it provides the film's visual music with a supplemental acoustic drive. It serves as well to ensure an element of continuity within the discontinuity of the shifting shots. In the turmoil of action, it serves as guarantor for the unity of the sequence. It lends the sequence a form on which the spectator can rely, even though, for the actors on the screen, nearly nothing is reliable.

Toward the end of the pursuit, one hears the shattering of glass and the sound of gunshots fired by the assassin at his adversary. Bourne groans softly as he tries to evade these attacks. At the moment that the SUV crashes, with aplomb, into the column, the music abruptly stops. For twenty seconds it is almost silent. We hear the braking of the other cars, and the sound of Bourne releasing first his seat belt and then the safety of his pistol. We hear the clank of his ruined vehicle and the tinkling of glass shards as he climbs out with a groan. As he moves toward the wrecked car, new music starts, overlaid by the murmuring of onlookers who are approaching the site of the accident and by the rising wail of sirens, audible from a distance. In this acoustic overlay, two of the film's crucial motif strands intersect. The sound of the sirens echoes the chaotic violence that the hero now leaves behind him. In contrast, the elegiac orchestral music, held back, as it were, by sluggish strains of the piano, intones what he has before him: the path to a young woman whose parents died violently years before. Bourne will confess to her that it was he who murdered her parents. This confession is part of his attempt not only to survive, but to come to terms with himself. What occurred and what will occur: it is *sound* that, with an incidental gesture, makes present this contrary motion as Bourne exits the grayness of the tunnel to face the grayness of the day.

Spaces of Time

This example makes plain just how much the visual architecture and visual music of films shape one another—and how much both, in the process, are underpinned by the dimension of sound. The sonic image space

that arises in this way is a time frame of a particular sort: a space that extends much further than that which appears within it; a time that stretches
far beyond what is visible and audible within it at the present moment.
This in itself is, admittedly, unremarkable. The same holds for any other
time and space of human action and experience. The world of a feature
film, however, is subject to its own laws. Its coordinates are shaped solely
by the motion of image and sound. Films execute their audiovisual movement between a definitive beginning and a definitive ending. What they
show and conceal, what they make heard and leave unheard, are determined by the choreography of their compositional medium. Their constellations expand the perceptibility of the world while drastically limiting it,
and they limit it while expanding it dramatically.

The mutual imbrication of filmic time and filmic space may be revealed at any tempo and at any degree of technical opulence. Rather
than an extravagant aesthetic of acceleration, powerful films may also
pursue a dramaturgy of slowing down. Rainer Werner Fassbinder's film
Katzelmacher (West Germany, 1969) was predominantly filmed in static
shots, and there is very little movement within the frame as well. The
monotonous lives, bristling with resentments, of a group of young men
and women are turned upside down by the arrival of a foreign guest
worker. The characters appear in shifting constellations in just a few settings. Dialogue is limited to meager exchanges. The roundelay of scenes
is broken up seven times by an intermezzo. In a rear courtyard bounded
by garages, two figures move toward the camera that is tracking back;
we hear Peer Raben's piano music, composed after Franz Schubert's
"Sehnsuchtswalzer." The film is composed like a rondo. It sketches, in
highly stylized fashion, the condition of a society held prisoner by the
force of its conventions.

In the film *Taste of Cherry* (*Ta'm-e gīlās*; Iran, France, 1997), director
Abbas Kiarostami has a man in a car circle Tehran for one and a half hours,
searching for someone who, for a good sum, is willing to bury him after his
suicide; we learn nothing about the motivations for the man's plan. There
is no music whatsoever, only background noises and the succession of
dialogues—a singular, open-ended searching movement that depicts a futile
life movement, though perhaps also an emboldening one.

The opening of Michelangelo Antonioni's film *L'Eclisse* (Italy, 1962)
likewise pursues an aesthetic of slowness. The camera moves reticently

within an elegant interior with drawn curtains. A couple, drained from a night of fighting, are together in the room, eyeing each other warily. There is no music. We hear the sound of a table fan, oscillating back and forth—a metaphor for the heat of the war of words they have just concluded and also for their perplexity about how to move forward. Otherwise, we hear only the footsteps of the restless Vittoria (Monica Vitti) and the movement of the small objects—an ashtray, a sculpture, a vase—that she touches, puts away, or rearranges. The camera lingers in close-up shots on the details of the interior. These objects, in their visual isolation, sing a silent song of their loss of meaning for the couple. This music of things expresses what, for the time being, remains unspoken: that things cannot go on the way they are. Like the young woman, the audience waits in anticipation of a moment of liberation, waits for the film to leave behind the narrowness of these quarters for the tumult of the city of Rome, waits as well for the woman to leave behind the narrowness of her life for the turbulence of a new affair. The film's final scene amounts to an inversion of the hesitant beginning. After Vittoria's affair with the young stockbroker Piero (Alain Delon) has run aground, the film spends seven minutes returning to places in the neighborhood where the couple used to meet. We see streets, corners, façades, and plazas—glimpses of locations, seemingly chosen at random, that are no longer sites of a shared life. In a documentary *gestus*, the film lingers in the waning daylight in a particular space, now devoid of the magnetism of Vittoria and Piero's mutual attraction. There are no voices to be heard, only the diffuse sounds of the nearly deserted suburb. The orchestral music (by Giovanni Fusco) accompanying this visual aria to lost love begins with a static or *ritardando* tempo, but culminates, as night falls, in an expressive gesture. After the spaces of the film's story have been revisited, all that remains is the echo of ambient sound.

Higher Rhythm[4]

The rhythmics of a film are invariably an admixture of elements. They arise from an interaction of their visible and audible aspects. The unity of sound and image in the film process, as Theodor W. Adorno and Hanns

Eisler observe in their book *Composing for the Films*, must be understood on the basis of the heterogeneity of visual and acoustic rhythms. It is only through the interference of these divergent movements that the "higher rhythm" of the total film emerges. For this reason, the authors propose an extension of the concept of montage beyond the domain of the image: "If the concept of montage, so emphatically advocated by Eisenstein, has any justification, it is to be found in the relation between the picture and the music. . . . This is dictated by the divergence of the media in question and the specific nature of each."[5] This comprehensive view of film composition pertains not only to the relationship between a succession of images and the music that is layered beneath it, however; it comprises all forms of a film's acoustic motion as well. Image and sound enter into the most varied amalgamations. Just as the movement of images and movement within the image may relate either synchronously or asynchronously to one another, interferences of image and sound may be organized in a harmonic or dissonant, a contrasting or complementary, manner, not to mention the symmetries and asymmetries, sequences and overlays, that may be contained within just the soundtrack. A film's audiovisual higher rhythm is a polyphonic composition even where image and sound seem to speak consistently with one voice.

This temporal organization is constitutive of the mutual entanglement, discussed in the previous chapter, of a film's virtual space and the real space in which it is presented. The filmic sound space is a component of the film's ambient sound; its time frame is a figure of its space-time. Everything that happens happens within a space that is happening; every action that is carried out is carried out within a formative time. Every film projects its own space within its own time. Its architecture of sound and image works hand in hand with its music of image and sound.

Explosion

Reflecting on the architecture *of* film is an entirely different matter than a consideration of architecture *in* film, even if this latter endeavor inevitably leaves its traces on the former. Something analogous is true about the topic of this chapter. My reflections on the music *of* film have touched again and again on the music *in* films, although the latter is not my primary concern. In both cases it is a matter of fundamental formal dimensions of films' audiovisual composition that are present even when—such as in the Bakersfield scene from *North by Northwest* or through long stretches of *Taste of Cherry*—a film stays away from interiors of buildings and has no musical accompaniment. In the final passage of Antonioni's *Zabriskie Point*, however, it all comes together: a building is exploded and with it the filmic space of action that had prevailed up to this point. There are visual fireworks as well, accompanied by evocative music.

At the film's conclusion, the young woman (Daria Halprin), having heard on the car radio that her friend has been shot by the police, imagines the explosion of a luxurious house nestled in the rocky outcropping of a hill outside of Phoenix, Arizona, the setting of some earlier scenes. Here the managers of the Sunnydunes Development Corporation are planning an absurd residential complex in the desert, a landscape constructed, in one of the film's earlier passages, as an anticapitalist paradise. The political and emotional antagonisms of the film's plot are discharged in the filmic realization of this revenge fantasy, achieving full autonomy from the film's narrative development, with no pretense whatsoever of psychological plausibility. At once abstract and decidedly concrete, the sequence sublates the predictable course of events. For more than five minutes, the film gives itself up to the pure vortex of its own appearing. The explosion repeats, at normal speed and with realistic acoustics, thirteen times in total, the repetitions coming in increasingly quick succession, the shots moving in closer and closer, showing the explosion from various vantage points. Again and again, items from the disintegrating home tumble in super slow motion through the image, propelled by the explosion. The passage is accompanied by music that pulsates aimlessly at first, then builds to an excessive eruption. As if the director had taken the pyrotechnic vocabulary of Adorno's *Aesthetic Theory* at its word, what occurs is an uprising of space and time against their economic deformation. The products of the world of commodities transform into sculptural objects that, cut loose from any utility, emancipate themselves. As if swimming underwater, household objects fly through the air with an unhurried momentum, the array creating a performance without performers, a happening in which nothing happens, in which nothing retains a stable form. A *natura naturans* now unbound by gravity erupts ominously and enchantingly out from behind the *natura naturata* and all the power of disposition that the latter underpins.

But it is not only objects that leave their established places behind; the film itself abandons the space of its story, before briefly immersing itself in its narrative landscape once again, at the very end. It presents dance theater without human actors, affording the audience something that otherwise only the spectacle of the natural landscape can offer: the possibility, from within the interpreted world, of leaving the interpreted world behind for a while.

3

FILM AS IMAGE

People Waiting

One-fifth of the way into the film *Perpetuum Mobile* by the Mexican director Nicolás Pereda (Mexico, Canada, 2009), we see Gabino, a slim young man with unkempt hair (Gabino Rodríguez), and his corpulent mother (Teresa Sánchez) sitting on an enormous sofa. It is a Sunday. They are waiting. More than half of the image is filled by the bare wall above the sofa. The mother sits with slumped shoulders, the son slouches in a nearly lying position. They are waiting for Gabino's brother to arrive for lunch. Their resigned body postures reveal that they are waiting in vain once again and that they know it. Traffic noises can be heard from outside. The scene runs for almost two minutes. Mother and son stare straight ahead, exchange a few words, sigh, and go back to staring. In these motionless intervals, movement is discernible only in their glances. The apathy of the figures is matched by an apathy of the filmic image. Unmoved, it captures their hopeless perseverance. It lets the audience wait along with the protagonists. The take gives the audience time to linger on the view of the scene, which in its muted colors gives the impression of a photorealist painting. The movement of the film is concentrated in a nearly stationary image.

Frequently in films, image movement appears to come to a standstill or does so in fact, either because movement *in* the image nearly or completely ceases or because the motion *of* the image is frozen for a moment. Yet just as silence in a piece of music represents an element of its sound, stasis in a film is a mode of image movement. No matter how closely film may approximate its siblings in the family of image forms and the pictorial arts, it remains a loner among them, even if its kinship with them is undeniable. Films cannot be reduced to a type of moving architecture with sound, nor to a type of music that plays with light—rather, they are *movies*, moving pictures. Of course, this particular image character of films was discussed throughout the first two chapters as well. As a nonliteral form of architecture and a nonliteral form of music, the cinematic film represents a decidedly real and quite specific form of the image.

Pictorial Appearing

Unlike other forms of representation, images are not primarily objects of saying, but of showing. They are renderings that present a variety of visible relations within the area of a surveyable surface. They reveal only constellations that are accessible to the eye, constellations in which the widest diversity of meaningful relations is arrayed. This image vision realizes a particular way of seeing-as: not the simple sort that is everywhere in force, in which something is merely perceived, whether accurately or erroneously (an object as a ball, a tree as a ghost, scenery as inviting), but rather the presentative variety that is present whenever a limited visual excerpt is comprehended as a *presentation* of something (a person, a landscape, a mood, an art movement, or a color harmony). Within their proper sphere, images show something that comes into appearance only in them, no matter how much or how little they may reference situations outside of their pictorial appearing.

As Richard Wollheim has insightfully established, there is always a "twofold attention" at play in the perception of images: an attention to the pictorial surface, that is, to the wide range of appearances visible within the boundaries of a two-dimensional area and, at the same time, an attention to what is presented in the way that this pictorial surface is organized. Gottfried Boehm sums up this doubling as an "iconic difference."[1] What comes into view in this schema may be "representational" or "nonrepresentational" references—ones that refer to conditions in the real world or in an imagined one, or else references in which the image object manifests aspects of its own composition. Whether one or the other mode is more prominent, one thing holds true: an image presents itself— thereby presenting *something*—to its observers. The artistic image in particular dramatizes this twofold relationship. It exhausts the potential of images. It makes *its own* appearing into the scene of *an* appearing, which always remains dependent on the intensity of *its own* appearing.

How an image appears and what appears in it always depend, in part, on the framework in which it is presented and the use to which it is put by its observers. Most images are not created to be perceived in relation to art, nor are they suited for it. They serve purposes of information or identification, representation or decoration, devotion or remembrance, agitation or advertisement, diagnosis or forensics, and many others besides (often serving several of these functions at once). Moreover, depending on the context of its use, quite disparate features may assume significance within the same image. Yet, however they are comprehended, as pictorial presentations they thrive on a tension between what they show and how they show it. Whether this tension becomes evident or not and, if so, to what degree it does, are of little consequence. As a rule, no one agonizes over the relationship between the manner and the object of representation when glancing at the pictures in the politics or sports section of the daily paper. For the most part, in such cases, what an image shows is established by conventions of image production as well as image perception. However, the interplay between the way it presents itself to the eye and what it presents in its visibility is implicit, at least, in every image. Anyone looking for this interplay from an analytical or aesthetic standpoint can find it everywhere. To be an image—to be comprehended as an image—means to be a potential site of divided attention.

However this plays out in terms of the production and reception of images, the latter create conditions for seeing and understanding that are separate and suspended from the body-centered conditions of perception that prevail in other contexts. This situation is fundamentally different from the intellectual operations of an imagination *detached* from the image, the so-called mental pictures that can range far beyond what is present in the moment, without ever existing in the exterior world. The material image that appears on walls or screens, on paper and other displays, in contrast, *is* present. In its two-dimensional space, it presents references that transcend their context. It makes itself visible in its sensuousness. In its physicality, it allows the observer to see beyond the physical world. Within its borders, it opens up a zone of the visible that makes ways of seeing—and thus of meaning—accessible to any observer, and potentially to the public at large. It makes possibilities of perception apparent and variegates them in the multiplicity of its forms. It allows us to see the act of seeing and thus to be sighted in a particular way. The imagination of an image is articulated imagination.

All of this applies to the filmic image as well. As a form of the pictorial, it shares the fundamental character of the image as described thus far. Through its motion combined with sound, however, it transforms the spatial and temporal relations of perception that govern still images. Its pictorial appearing conjoins with the dimensions of the architectonic and the musical that we reviewed in the previous chapters. This admixture is responsible for the fact that film is capable of imposing *its* movement on its audience in more radical a fashion than any other presentation or any other art of presentation—whether it be a matter of texts, conversations, speeches, forms of music, theater, and dance, or any other sort of performance. More radically than any form of music alone, it sets the audience's time; more radically than any other form of the merely pictorial, it takes the audience along in its space, which is at once determinate and indeterminate. More radically than any other form of the pictorial, it leads its spectators into a zone of imagination, even when—in fact, particularly when—its vistas are produced from photographs of the real world.

Image and Movement

Let us return for a moment to the beginning of the transitional sequence from *Zabriskie Point*. It starts with a shot of a steer that gazes somewhat dolefully out at the audience. The animal stands on a patch of grass, the barest suggestion of a pasture against a broad, light-blue surface. The words "FEDERALLY INSPECTED MEATS" can be read below the pictogram. The image moves slowly to the left in front of the static camera while in the lower half of the screen the top of a truck moves rapidly to the right. The meat truck with the steer emblem then exits the frame, leaving an unobstructed view of a wall mural depicting a farmer throwing pumpkins and corncobs to fat, black pigs from the back of a cart. Cut. Close shot of the jovial farmer. Cut. The camera completes a pan across the painted scene. Cut. We see the pickup with the two students drive past this landscape, now recognizable as a work of naïve façade painting. Cut. Tires screeching, the pickup makes a turn around the building, which is now seen to be a warehouse for meat products. The side of the building that now becomes visible is also painted with grotesque scenes of country life from bygone times. Cut. The camera zooms in on a ragged figure being chased by a farmer whose pig he is trying to steal. Cut. The camera, mounted on the back of the pickup, travels past the painted façade of the warehouse.

All in the space of sixteen seconds, this is a large number of image situations at once. The significance of the steer pictogram is automatically accessible to anyone: it is an advertisement for meat. The status of the painted landscape poses more of a puzzle, in part because it is not immediately recognizable as a mural, but also because it conforms to the genre of the rustic idyll, but presented in the style of the comics. Given enough time, however, one would arrive at the calculus of these scenes, too: the industry's typical whitewashing of meat production. The image composition of the film, on the other hand, is far more complex. The images within the image, as well as the surface on which they appear, only reveal themselves in successive fashion. Little by little, it becomes apparent what is foreground and what is background. The image movement presents the space of the city as a moving image space in which it remains opaque what is functional and what is a façade. (Shortly after, we see an exceedingly kitschy promotional film for an absurd construction project in the desert.) The overlay of image levels, as well as their shift into increasing opacity—an opacity also of the filmic image events—provokes a "seeing vision," as Max Imdahl termed what he deemed a central dimension of viewing artistic images.[2]

At the same time, however, this brief passage is a demonstration of the particular constitution of the filmic image itself. With the image on the meat truck, which moves past the camera *within* this sequence, as well as the painted landscape *along which* the camera moves, this scene shows up the transgressive character of the filmic image. What was seen inside the image one moment has passed to the outside the next; what was outside pushes its way in. The boundaries of the moving image are porous. What happens on the screen always references what has already happened there, what will happen, or what could have happened. The realities of filmic appearing are perpetually surrounded by the possibilities—realized and unrealized—of what can unfold with sound and image. As André Bazin puts it, "The screen is not a frame like that of a picture but a mask [*cache*] which allows only a part of the action to be seen."[3]

Yet with still images, too, their visibility stands in contrast to what remains invisible in them. Every image shows only a detail, an excerpt. And each image behaves differently with regard to this excerpt character. Moreover, every type of image deals differently with the boundaries of the image. Many paintings show only their own cosmos; it would be pointless to ask what lies outside the frame. They show what they show, and that is that. What the painting does not reveal is left invisible once and for all. The subject and its realization are in the hands of the painter, the product of his whim. He decides what to place within the surface area of his picture and how it will be situated. As much as the perception of the observer, before a painted scene, may at times be inveigled into extending or filling in, in imagination, the context in which the image is situated, what the image makes manifest is *its own* perspective on what is visible within *it*. This perspective is often indifferent with regard to any concrete exterior—even when what the image presents is a well-known natural or urban landscape. What extends beyond the boundaries of the image motif—above, below, and to the side—remains irrelevant for its fashioning as a painterly object. Even where particular paintings expressly draw attention to their excerpt character, they do not refer to conditions beyond their image frame. Rather, they place their space, the space internal to the image, in a complex relationship to the space in which they are being observed.

Yet another dynamic is at play in the case of paintings that appear in series—one thinks of Giotto's fresco cycle in the Arena Chapel in Padua, the experiments in painting by Barnett Newman that go by the title *Who's Afraid of Red, Yellow and Blue,* or Gerhard Richter's *October 18, 1977,* a series of paintings based on police photographs that bring into presence the death of members of the Red Army Faction in Stammheim prison. In these instances, the relationship of one image to the next, and the transitions between them, are wholly different than in the process that constitutes the filmic image. We must make the transition between our observation of one and our observation of another and the next; *they* do not flow one into another. And yet, while clearly we cannot refer to movement *in* the image or movement of the image space *itself* in works of painting, even here there is motion of the image, in the literal sense. The art of cinema is distinguished from the other pictorial arts solely by the *nature* of its processuality. Stationary images are processual by virtue of the interaction of their internal components. To follow these relations—and in particular their "seeing vision"—in perception demands that the observer go along with the inner motion in the spatial arrangement of the settings and figures, the use of light, the coloration, the application of paint, and other painterly gestures. Moreover, even motionless images can represent movement and can, at will, either enhance or reduce the drama in what is being represented. The inner temporality of the static image, however, including its inner spatiality, has quite a different disposition than that of the moving image.

As in its relationship to architecture and music, film is to be distinguished from the picture not least by a difference in the corporeality that informs their perception. The picture permits a lingering view, in which the time devoted to observation and the distance between the observer and the pictorial object can be varied as desired. The cinematic film allows no such variation: it subjects its spectators, both physically and "metaphysically," to its own audiovisual movement, which can culminate in an assault on their physical and psychic equilibrium.

Photography and Film

Painted images present their own cosmos, whether they make reference to conditions in the real world or only put their own interior motion on display. Photographs, on the other hand, present a temporal and spatial excerpt of a reality that extends beyond the boundaries of the image: something that was there—in front of the camera aimed in its direction—and has left behind an enduring trace here—in the photographic image. "A painting *is* a world; a photograph is *of* the world," as Stanley Cavell puts it.[4] Putting aside, for a moment, the thoroughly staged image motifs of advertising and art, a photograph always raises a twofold question about what lies outside the image. The question pertains to the image's points of reference, on one hand, and, on the other, to the demarcation of its boundaries. What can be seen *in* the image is an arrangement of objects or of circumstances that have brought about the pictorial appearing. What *the* image shows is an excerpt of the real; it refers to a point in space and time in the external world. That is why it corresponds at the same time to an undefined multiplicity that is cropped out on all sides by the framing of the image. The photographic image's reference to reality depends on the fact that everything captured within it is part of a network of connections that exceeds its frame. Faced with a photographic image, we are confronted, at the same time, with what it does not present to our view.

This is an utterly different outside than the one with which films maintain an ongoing exchange. The situation is different if only because films—not only documentaries, but often enough fiction films as well—are predicated on the realistic potential of the photographic reference to the world (as I will discuss in more detail in chapter 6). Above all, however, the situation is different because the action of a film image can, at any time and in any direction, transcend the frame of what has been visible up to that point and maintain the presence of what lies beyond the visible through the effects of sound. The horizon of a film forms and transforms by way of the glimpses it allows into its space, as well as the movements it performs within it. Part of this unsteady framing, which underlies all filmic action, is the unsteady view that it offers its observers. Within the boundaries of the screen, the moving image is continually exceeding its own boundaries. It represents a constant variation of disembodied focal points. The photographic image, in contrast, fixes *one* focal point (or else integrates multiple ones into a new view). It holds something firmly within its frame that inexorably draws the attention of the observer. While film lets itself and its observers go, photography blocks the passage—or the leap—to the sidelines of the image. Film does not tolerate lingering with one conclusively fixed perspective—except in those moments in which it interrupts its flow with freeze frames or, as in the scene from *Perpetuum Mobile*, verges on the state of immobile images.

Another Trip

In *Perpetuum Mobile*, after Gabino and his mother have given up waiting, they sit silently at lunch. The young man takes his plate and leaves the table without a word. Cut. Gabino and his partner are on the road in a shabby moving truck. Both of them are telling stories of dreams in which dogs play the leading role. The trip lasts two minutes, twenty-one seconds. The camera, mounted in front of the vehicle's windshield, first shows a side shot of Gabino behind the wheel. In the middle of the passage, as the passenger tells his story, the camera changes angles; now it is aimed at him from an analogous position. During the trip, indistinct fragments of Mexico City can be seen through a narrow opening in the side window. We hear driving sounds, the rush of traffic, and, once, the voice of a street vendor. Our view of the protagonists remains indistinct as well, however, because the entire sequence is dominated by the spectacle of the reflections of the urban space the two are passing through. The silhouettes of trees, telephone lines and poles, and street lamps move in a filmic image within the filmic image. Our view of the truck's occupants is interrupted again and again by the shifting sunlight as it falls into the vehicle. The surface of the windshield is blindingly bright for a moment, then almost black, then nearly a solid sky blue until again we can recognize the reflection of the surroundings that pass as shadows from bottom to top, just as the mirror of the windshield becomes transparent again, permitting a view of the two figures.

As in the opening credits of *North by Northwest* that we considered at the end of chapter 1, what appears on the screen here is a second glassy screen upon which events that lie outside of the camera's focus are played out. Observers see a moving image that presents a moving image—and in this way makes perceptible the presence of the space of the metropolis, which is otherwise largely absent from the picture. In the film's story, the scene also functions as a metaphor for the two protagonists' aimless drifting. In addition, the two fixed shots of a moving object take up the motif of the picture within a picture, which also plays a major role in painting. Here, however, it is produced through a photographic technique that engenders its own forms of the image—and thus also of the picture within a picture.

However, "photographic technique" by no means signifies the same thing in the case of film as in the case of photography. To illustrate this point, let me pause this sequence from Pereda's film on a few arbitrary frames. In many of these stills, fragments of the city that the protagonists are driving through are recognizable through one or the other of the side windows; behind the transparent screen of the windshield, either the driver or the front passenger can be seen in a particular posture. On the surface of the windshield, objects from the environs are reflected, projected by daylight onto the display within the image. What we see are photographic images that maintain a striking relationship with the space outside the focus of the camera. We see objects that have found their way in front of the camera, and at the same time we see the conditions that have captured them, by means of reflected light, on the surface of the object immediately in front of them. In other stills, by contrast, we see nearly monochrome areas of color: almost black, yellowish white, or blue. They come close to the abstract pictorial forms familiar from modernist painting. Other examples of the freeze-frame images exhibit various mixing ratios of representational and nonrepresentational imagery. Yet because it is a matter of photographic recording in each case, they all share the *gestus* of representing something within their fixed frame, the assertion that in a particular place, for one split second, it was as they show it.

Now I will let the film run again. Right away we are subjected to a continuous stream of images with constantly shifting light and color, as well as a sound sequence of speech and noise. There is no single point in time at which we can pause. We linger, rather, at and within the present of an audiovisual process that transposes the external realities of its production onto the spatial and temporal horizon of its own phenomenal motion. Films and photographs make completely different promises to their observers—and the two arts conduct themselves completely differently with regard to the promises they make.

The Promise of Photography

The photographic image is bound through its technology to a simple gesture from which all of its miracles issue. It is distinguished by its realistic apparency,[5] which may be realized or unrealized. The photographic image contains a promise to be the evidence of a present that is past: a constellation of objects that were actually at a particular place at the moment the image came into being. Yet by no means do photographic images always keep this promise. It is possible to interfere so forcefully with the configuration of the objects visible in the image that there is simply no longer any particular place or time to which the image refers. Images that are considered photographic present themselves as the optical capture of a past moment. In this *gestus* lies the specific potential of the medium of photography, which is also exploited by those photographic images that break the promises that they contain, whether openly or secretly, fully or only in part.

What makes an image photographic is its origin in recordings made via some sort of camera lens. This is what distinguishes this form of the image from the products of computer graphics that do not derive from a photographic process. Photographic images are ones in whose birth the light of the world has played a causal role. They present the trace of an order of things that once existed beyond the camera, although much may remain invisible that could have been seen, had one been present, and much may be revealed that would, by necessity, have remained invisible without the camera's gaze.

Multiple parameters play their various, disparate roles in the production of these images: the eye of the photographer, the type of lens, the exposure time, the use of various aperture settings and filters, the camera angle, the moment of the shot, the focus on fortuitous or elaborately staged subjects and circumstances, the type of developing, processing, and postprocessing, the possibilities for montage and composition within the image, including the realization of the image in a particular format and a particular material medium. Like all images, photographic ones are artifacts through and through. They never merely reflect; rather, they construct a viewpoint, their own viewpoint. Like every image, they present their own configuration of elements, by means of which they refer to circumstances beyond the image—only in this case, that configuration is already given. But only very particular given circumstances are extracted and presented as an image. Even within its boundaries, a photograph shows only what has been highlighted and retained in the way it was shot and processed. Only here can we identify what the photograph identifies. The photographic image permits us to see *one* past reality, but only in the present of *its own* reality. The specific reference of the photographic image remains dependent on the opacity of its appearing.[6]

Digital production and processing of images have not changed anything fundamentally in this regard. After all, interventions in the original image generated by the camera were always possible in the darkroom; computer graphics programs have merely greatly expanded the options. In terms of photography, the digital age has, for this reason, been characterized by a heightened uncertainty with regard to the status of photographic images—an ontological blurriness with which advertising and segments of fine art photography have long operated. How to assess this blurriness and how to manage it depend, in essence, on the contexts in which the photographic images are used. It is part of the ethos of journalistic photography to capture situations precisely as they occurred at a particular place. In art photography, on the other hand, everything is permissible that will produce a powerful image. Composition, transposition, transfiguration: *anything goes.*

This is why, in speaking of the photographic medium, it is appropriate to refer to a realistic gesture, but not to a thoroughgoing realism on the part of its images.[7] What constitutes photography's specific appearing is that it makes an excerpt of the world visible. Frequently bound up with this apparency is its claim to reproduce something that was present in front of the camera at the moment of the shot. If it was really like the photograph presents it, this claim is realized; if not, it remains unrealized. If this claim is asserted through the context in which an image is presented— say, in news or reportage—but the image does not deliver on the claim, then it is in service to a rhetoric of deception. The photographic image becomes part of a lie through its presentation. (A photographic image *alone*, independent of the particular context in which it is employed, is not capable of lying, since it does not, in and of itself, *say* anything that could be true or false.) This claim, though it is suggested by the photographic gesture, does not have to be raised, however. It can, in various ways, be undermined, disrupted, thematized, reflected, or completely rejected. This is by no means always the case in fine art photography, but these approaches are increasingly prevalent—one thinks of the photographic picture-puzzles of Andreas Gursky or Beate Gütschow. It is not uncommon to encounter compositions whose pictorial presentation does not correspond to any situation in the real world. Photography's promise to refer to configurations of the real can be kept most saliently precisely where it is broken: where the scene in the image does not correspond to any situation in the real world.

Image Analysis

The status of photography from the perspective of film and what this means for the ethos of film is a central motif in Michelangelo Antonioni's film *Blow-Up* (UK and Italy, 1966). *Blow-Up* is concerned with the power and powerlessness of the photographic image and the obsessions associated with it, to which even much of the theory of photography and film is not immune. At the center of the film, the main character, a nameless photographer (David Hemmings), is preoccupied with the analysis of a series of photographs that he shot in a park that morning, rather by chance. (The photos are black-and-white; the film is in color.) The photographer becomes increasingly absorbed by the shots he has just developed, in which he comes to believe he has discovered a murder scene. Particularly at the beginning of this sequence, the film becomes an object lesson in the ontology of both static and moving images.

The setting is the photographer's loft studio. We see him from the back, sitting on a sofa and smoking. His gaze—and that of the audience—falls on two large-format, black-and-white photos, fresh from the darkroom, which he has attached to a beam. Cut. We see the photographer from the front, staring at the images in a contemplative pose. He gets up and moves closer to the photographs. Cut. The first photo is seen in close-up; it fills the entire screen. We see a woman and a man standing in front of a fence that encircles the park; the woman holds his hand and pulls him in her direction. (We have already seen the scene at the beginning of the film, in the filmic image, from the perspective of the photographer as he takes his pictures.) After two seconds, the camera pans to the right, from the first image to the second. It shows the woman and the man in a tight embrace.

For three seconds, this image fills the screen. The camera pans back to the first image, lingers there briefly, then pans back to the second image again. In the course of this back-and-forth, the camera zooms closer to the two figures in the picture. Our view of the photos follows the photographer's eye movements as he studies them. This movement is accompanied by the sound of rustling leaves, which could be heard in the park as the pictures were taken. We see through the eyes of the photographer and hear him remembering the circumstances at the site that morning. (Or perhaps he is hallucinating the sound; he didn't sleep the night before, and as the film progresses he is increasingly under the influence of drugs, lending his reconstruction of events a rather dubious character.) Cut. The camera is positioned at an angle behind the second image; the photographer is seen in front of the image, studying it. As he moves closer to the image, the camera pans so that it is now completely behind the picture, which again fills the entire screen. Illuminated by studio spotlights, the image remains visible in this shot, though fainter and in a laterally reversed view. At the same time, we see the shadows cast on the image by the head of the ob-server moving in front of it. Cut. The photographer stands directly facing the two images that now reflect, more intensely than before, the light of the studio lamps aimed at them.

Multiple filmic aphorisms about the relationship between photography and film are contained in the forty seconds of this passage. The photogra-pher seeks to learn what is behind the mystery that his photos might possi-bly pose. Yet behind the image is only—the image again. Anything that his photograph can show about the situation in the park it can show only on its surface. The glare of reflected light prominent on the front surface of both photos reveals their status as material objects that—unlike the cam-era's viewfinder that engendered them—refuse transparency. Only within the confines of the image do they refer to a reality that is external to the image, a reality that is absent in space and time. They disclose nothing but *their own* view of this reality. The same holds true for the individual filmic image—the still—inasmuch as it originates in photographic production. But it does not apply to filmic image movement. The latter can always take us behind the views that it has previously afforded (or move past them, as in the scene from *Zabriskie Point* commented on above). Image movement can change and combine times and spaces at random. This it can do because its architecture produces its own image time and its own image space, in which every shot exists in the context of many other shots, and every focal point communicates with all of the other focal points. Thus arises a network of relations among the various views, which, taken as a whole, does not represent any situation external to the image even if every *image* of the film, in isolation, refers to such situations.

The decisive difference between the photographic and the filmic image is made manifest in *Blow-Up* in the moment when the camera moves back and forth between the two photos in a point-of-view shot. This movement forces the spectator to follow what is visible in the picture in a predetermined temporal operation. The particular temporality of the filmic image is demonstrated in the process of observing two photographs that precisely do not correspond to this form of the temporal. The motion of the filmic image does not *re*produce a past spatial and temporal state of affairs; it *pre*scribes for its observers the timing of their observation. The primary temporal mode of photography is the preterite tense: it conserves a moment that is past. Film's primary temporal mode, in contrast, is the present tense: it displays the present of its appearing in sound and image.[8]

This present that unfolds within the space of the cinema—and only there—occurs regardless of whether and to what degree the succession of images refers to situations that are external to the image. *Many films* make promises of this sort, but *film* does not. Film promises something entirely different. Film guarantees its spectators that it will take them along into the time and space of its moving present. Whether it is a fiction film, a documentary, or a mixture of the two; whether it is an experimental film, an animation, or an essay film; whether it has its origins in analogue or digital processes (or a combination)—all film genres share this *gestus*. Even if the *degree* to which this promise can be kept is highly variable—depending on the type and quality of the films in question—it cannot be broken, because it is inscribed in the formal constitution of the cinematic film.

The Promise of Film

The image analysis carried out in *Blow-Up* is far from over with the end of the scene discussed above. It is just the beginning of a longer process of enlarging—blowing up—the two original images. The next picture to be developed shows a close-up of the man and women in a tight embrace.

The woman's gaze is averted from her partner. She gazes transfixed into a space outside of the image frame, in the direction of the fence that surrounds the park, which was visible in the larger detail. It is this gaze that sets off the process by which the photographer, like a detective, seeks to coax from his photos the truth about what happened.

This process will later culminate in a remarkable dialogue. "I saw a man killed this morning," the photographer says to his neighbor, a young woman who visits him in the studio. "Where?" she asks. "Shot. In some sort of park."—"Are you sure?"—"He's still there."—"Who was he?"—"Someone."—"How did it happen?"—"I don't know. I didn't see."—"You didn't see."—"No." The photographer did not see how it—the supposed murder—happened because all he has seen are the traces that the event left behind in his photographs. (Even the body, which he believes he saw with his own eyes when he was at the site at night *without* a camera will have vanished upon his next visit to the park.) "Shouldn't you call the police?" the young woman asks. In lieu of an answer, the photographer shows her an extremely enlarged detail from one of the photos. This photographic image is the last one he is left with, the others having been stolen along with the negatives. "That's the body" is his only comment. Looks like one of Bill's paintings," the woman replies, astonished. "Yes."

Bill's latest paintings were seen at the start of the film. They are abstract, diffuse image surfaces, gray on gray, that are scattered with dots and lines in open dispersion. As the comparison made in the dialogue suggests, when a photograph is forced to bear witness to what was before the camera beyond the recognizable configurations contained in the photograph, the latter dissolves into a field of abstract markings. It becomes ornamental; it loses its quality as evidence for a situation outside of the image. The photographer's obsessive enlargement processes cause the referential character of his images to implode. Photographs, if they keep any promise at all, keep only *their own* promise: that something was really there that has been captured in them—and only in *them*—and is now visible there. A photograph is always an excerpt, a detail, always bound to its particular view and its attestation to a present that is now past. Films, on the other hand, achieve a permanent, or at least permanently potential, transgression of everything that is visible at any moment within the boundaries of the screen. Films operate in an intangible world even when that world exhibits many of the features of the familiar one.

Blow-Up carries out the investigation into its own image forms primarily from an attitude of skepticism. As different from each other as their operations might be, neither photography nor film can lay claim to the reality that appears in them or that they invent. Yet, in the end, film's mistrust of its two underlying media turns into a form of irreligious trust. Now the insufficient reliability of the photographic image as well as the filmic moving image appears as an emblem of the worldliness of both photography and film. After all, there is much in the natural, historical, and social world to which we are bound, and much that defines us, which we can never fully grasp. We can neither conclusively determine, nor even *want* to determine, what will move us and what we want to move us. Film in particular demonstrates how absurd—not to mention futile—such desire would be. With its own motion, film demonstrates what it means to be subject to concealment within openness, transience within time, happenstance within action, ignorance within knowledge, being-moved within movement. Whatever a film promises, rightly or wrongly, it keeps the promise to be a variation on the human being-in-the-world—and thus a variety of the same.

Another Ending

On the morning of the plot's second day, after a night of revelry, the photographer in *Blow-Up* makes his way to the park, with his camera, to verify the existence of the body. (The audience has seen only rather peculiar *filmic* images of it, shot at night.) But the body is not there. Dispirited and helpless, he looks around the scene of the supposed drama. He takes no more photographs. The heat of the search for the truth behind his pictures is extinguished. He meanders through the grounds. In his right hand, he holds the camera loosely by the strap. Again he comes upon a boisterous group wearing colorful costumes and carnivalesque face paint who made their anarchic presence felt at the start of the film as well. They congregate around a tennis court that appeared on the screen in passing during the photographer's first walk through the park, although in that scene, the sound of the players' rally was audible. But now, a woman and a man from the group begin a pantomimed tennis match, observed by the photographer who stands against the high chain-link fence that borders the court. The spectators follow the game with equally pantomimed reactions, drawing an easy smile from the photographer, an expression he has not displayed in the entire film up to this point. His gaze follows the back-and-forth of the imaginary rally. Now the camera joins in, following the imaginary ball in a pan interrupted by close-ups showing the fervor of the players. The male player mimes the movement of a vigorous return shot that sends the "ball" high over the fence—and it is the camera that follows the immaterial object in its flight to the green surface of the adjacent lawn.

At this point, the film fully succumbs to the fictions of the pantomime. With gestures, the young woman appeals to the photographer to retrieve the ball for her. Watched by the whole group, the onlooker, camera still in hand, runs to where the imaginary ball has landed. Arriving at the spot, he lays his camera in the grass. He picks up the "ball," weighs it in his hand, and vigorously pitches it toward the tennis court, following the imagined object with his eyes. Pensively, he remains standing and watches as the game resumes. At the same time, we *hear* the sound of the nonexistent rally: the film reinforces its own fiction even on the acoustic level. The subsequent shot, the film's final one, shows the photographer from a bird's-eye view, standing on the empty lawn. He walks to his camera, picks it up, takes a few steps, then stands and watches the tennis match as the film's title melody (composed by Herbie Hancock) starts, until his figure is erased and the insert "THE END" appears.

It is, first of all, the *film* that relates in a remarkable way, here, to the reality of the story it is telling. In image and in sound it goes along with the imagination of the pantomime performance. This is particularly clear from the movement with which the camera makes present the trajectory of the "ball" as it flies out of the court. Since there is no ball, it certainly cannot follow its flight. The camera does not trace the course; it plots it. Nor is it the movement of any of the characters' gaze that the camera follows. Certainly, the pan executed by the camera might be seen as the representation of a subjective movement of the gaze. But then the camera *tracks* the ball, trailing behind it as it rolls. By contrast, in the previous and subsequent shots we see that all of the figures watching the "ball" *remain standing*. Thus it cannot be *their* movement that accompanies the imaginary object. Indeed, within the world of the film, this is a matter of an *objective* take on an imaginary occurrence. The camera *itself*—and with it the film—enters into the reality imagined by the characters. The film makes their imagination its own. This, too, can be accomplished through movement of the filmic image. In the face of objective realities—in this case a mundane lawn—it can present unreal events. The real sound of the imaginary rally on the tennis court merely reinforces this transformation. Reality and unreality are blended and transposed; the invisible becomes visible, the inaudible, audible. In the cinema, one thing we can rely on is that we cannot always rely on our image of the real.

Secondly, the *character* of the photographer undergoes a transformation in this final sequence. After all, he also enters into the mimes' imagination. While heretofore the photographer had acted solely according to his own rules, now he takes part in a social game. For the first time in the film, he goes along with something that others want from him. His egocentric attitude begins to crumble. Up to this point, he has behaved like a junkie of the moment, for whom all that counts is the here and now. The whole time, the photographer has been fixated on fixing his images. By laying aside his camera at the end of the film, he parts ways with his *déformation professionnelle*. What takes place is at least a temporary transformation of the hero. He relinquishes comprehension. He gives up control. He lets what happens happen. He gains an insight that the film also expects of its viewers: that the predominant meaning of the appearing of images can lie in their impenetrability. And that is not all. He gains the outlook that every film demands of its viewers: only if they give themselves up to the events of the film will they be taken along to where only film can take them.

4

Film as Spectacle

Anarchy

At the end of the film *A Night at the Opera* (Sam Wood, USA, 1935), scenes unfold before and during a New York premiere of Verdi's *Il Trovatore* that grow increasingly absurd. The Marx Brothers—Groucho, Harpo, and Chico—sabotage the performance in order to force their favorites, the tenor Riccardo Baroni (Allan Jones) and the soprano Rosa Castaldi (Kitty Carlisle), to be allowed on stage—a ploy that ultimately succeeds. Groucho makes insulting comments to the audience while Harpo and Chico sow unrest in the orchestra; next the latter two mix with the actors on the stage, perpetrating mischief of all sorts. The theater director and a police sergeant don disguises in order to put an end to the goings-on, while the sergeant's men take up position backstage. The hullabaloo escalates when Harpo, fleeing from his pursuers, climbs up a piece of the stage set and clamors around the fly loft, causing a succession of different backdrops to rise and lower, while the ensemble tries desperately to sing over the chaos. Finally, after reducing the already tattered scenery to shreds, Harpo, defying gravity, runs up the remnants of the scenery flat and, while police and stage crew attempt to reach him in the rigging, swings on a trapeze to the main switch and turns off all the lights. The screen goes black. The music goes silent. A cry is heard. Then, after some backstage negotiations—carried out in the light again—the substituted singers bring the production to a triumphant end.

The anarchy of the action in this sequence corresponds to an anarchy that characterizes its cinematographic representation. The latter undermines any hierarchy of perspectives from which the unbridled events on the stage are made visible. The perspective of the opera audience is merely one among many viewpoints on the actions that are unfolding. The movie camera operates in front of, on, above, next to, and even (from the orchestra pit) below the stage. The rapidly changing views it generates do not privilege any one of these perspectives. They have no stable position at the site that constitutes the scene of the action. Nevertheless, the sequence of shots is governed by a clear calculation. It ratifies the chaos that the actions of the actors produce.

Not just *this* film, but *film as such* leaps around with its audience in a way that stage performance simply cannot do. Like theater, opera, and dance, film *is* a spectacle. All of these art forms are, for the most part, also visual and acoustic productions. They all reveal events in images. Each gives rise to its particular space. All are sustained by the delivery of their performers. But the spectacle of film obeys its own laws.

Division of Space, Again

Not only film, but the performing arts as well operate with a particular process of spatial division. The central difference here is obvious, however. In the theater and related arts, the audience and the performers *share* a space in which the performance takes place, a space that is subdivided by means of a stage or other markers. In the cinema, on the other hand, the spectators are subjected to a space in motion, one that is fundamentally inaccessible to their intervention. Erwin Panofsky refers to this difference when he defines the "specific possibilities of the new medium . . . as *dynamization of space* and, accordingly, *spatialization of time*," a lead that I have pursued at some length in the first two chapters.[1]

> In a theater, space is static, that is, the space represented on the stage, as well as the spatial relation of the beholder to the spectacle, is unalterably fixed. . . . With the movies the situation is reversed. Here, too, the spectator occupies a fixed seat, but only physically, not as the subject of an aesthetic experience. Aesthetically, he is in permanent motion as his eye identifies itself with the lens of the camera, which permanently shifts in distance and direction. And as movable as the spectator is, as movable is, for the same reason, the space presented to him. Not only bodies move in space, but space itself does, approaching, receding, turning, dissolving and recrystallizing as it appears through the controlled locomotion and focusing of the camera and through the cutting and editing of the various shots—not to mention such special effects as visions, transformations, disappearances, slow-motion and fast-motion shots, reversals and trick films. This opens up a world of possibilities of which the stage can never dream.[2]

What Panofsky highlights here is the disembodied point of view from which the cinema audience follows the occurring space of a film. Its perception is guided by a space formed of light and sound that unfolds as the events of the film unfold. Spectators participate in this space as "subjects of aesthetic experience." The changes of this space befall spectators from the inside out, independent of their bodily perspectives. They are not merely led, seeing, *into* an otherwise inaccessible space, as can also happen before a still image. They are led, seeing and hearing, *within* a space that exists solely in the time of sound and image movement.

There is no analogue in the theatrical sphere. In the theater as in all other sites of scenic performance (including music performed on stages or other podiums), all parties involved, whether actively or passively, are physically present in one and the same space. Theater can loosen the barrier between performance and audience, render it porous, or marginalize it to the point of invisibility: nonetheless, a divided space remains, albeit one that is physically shared by audience and performers. *Within this space*, movement takes place in a variety of ways, yet *the space itself* is not in motion. No matter how much movement might happen on the stage or how much the stage itself might move in certain cases, these processes always unfold within a space of action that is accessible to all in common, even if the different parties have completely different roles, in accordance with the conventions of the particular performance.

The spectators in the cinema also share a social space, but as corporeal subjects they are excluded from the space of the presentation. Collectively, they are present at a presentation of absent situations and events. The process of the filmic division of space explored in the first chapter is a basic principle of the filmic moving image that determines the spatial and temporal configurations of the current and latent events on the screen. Certainly, traces of this principle are at work even in conventional stage action. The actors' entrances and exits as well as sounds and sound effects can evoke that space beyond what the audience can see on the stage, the space where a good deal of the subversive action at the end of *A Night at the Opera* plays out. Yet it is precisely this partitioning into "inside" and "beyond" the space of presentation that has no equivalent in film. Here every beyond is a potential inside and every inside a potential beyond, without these positions bearing any relation to the spatial or temporal position of the observers.

Virtuality

The gag with the rising and descending stage backdrops in *A Night at the Opera* reminds us that film and theater are not only arts of space and time; they both are pictorial arts as well. The way this gag is executed, however, underscores the divergence in how the two art forms direct the gaze—and thus makes evident the divergent character of their imagery. Theatrical space is, for the most part, also a space *of images* (in which filmic images may also play a role); filmic space, on the other hand, is always an *image space*. The latter constitutes and opens up a virtual space. In contrast to both the inner processuality of static, artistic images and the movement of images within an action on the stage, we have to do, here, with a *processing* space. It consists solely of the filmic movement of image and sound, and it ends with that. This is a space that can be explored only by seeing, hearing, and otherwise sensing.

Certainly, static images can also provide a view into a virtual space accessible only to the eye. Yet this space, along with the glimpse into it that the image enables, is unchanging. It is fixed, once and for all. It is only with the "architectonic" and "musical" organization of the moving image that the space of a single image is transposed into a dynamic image space that can cause different views to appear and disappear at any time. The various performing arts do not establish a virtual space of this sort. Their art consists in a transformation of real space into the space of dramatic fiction, producing a scenic imagination or other performance in motion, executed with the bodily presence of the respective actors.

Sculpturality

The particular spatiality of the filmic image is also illuminated by the particular plasticity that its shots can lend to (and thus also withhold from) the objects it represents. The opening scene of *L'Eclisse*, described in chapter 2, shows the couple, exhausted from a night of fighting, surrounded by the furnishings of a space that up to that point had been part of the life they shared together. Individual items—books, lamps, chairs, a fan, a figurine, a picture frame, a vase, an ashtray—are moved into the image frame from various perspectives, appearing now as foreign objects. Repositioning these objects with its shifting gaze, the camera highlights their position within the space of the action, in which they lead a curiously independent life. They take on a plastic quality: they are brought forth out of the center of the space that, for the couple that inhabits it together, no longer affords a center.

This option can be exploited in even more dramatic a fashion. Toward the end of *Zabriskie Point*, before the final episode with the luxury villa, the propeller plane stolen by the male lead is pursued by police cars, sirens wailing, when it lands at an airport in Los Angeles. An aerial shot follows the plane's evasive maneuvers. Two close-ups show police firing at the young man in the cockpit. The police sirens go silent. Another aerial shot. The camera circles the now-motionless airplane from above, completing a nearly 360-degree shot. The camera moves in closer and closer to its object, finally zooming in close to the cockpit. After a few additional close-ups taken from ground level, we see the lifeless pilot within.

As the camera travels around the plane, it appears as if the ground were turning itself before the camera's gaze, though it is the movement of the image itself that produces this effect. The airplane, painted with flower-power designs by the hero and his companion during its desert excursion, is displayed before our eyes like a sculpture. Now it becomes a sign of the futility of the rebellious act for which it has been employed, and of the abortive hopes of the student movement as well. The tracking shot around the airplane that has come to a standstill brings into presence the standstill of this movement.

Not only can films place the objects and figures that they present in a space of their own; they can set them in motion from the center outward, surround them, probe them optically. Film can lend a particular plasticity to the objects that appear in its image space; it can arrange them into installations and move about them as if in an art installation, because the camera can encounter these objects from any direction. It can make them appear within a space and it can make their space appear; it can set them in motion within its space and it can cause this space to move. Using mirrors—as in the finale of *The Lady from Shanghai* (Orson Welles, USA, 1948) or Rainer Werner Fassbinder's *World on a Wire* (*Welt am Draht*; West Germany, 1973)—it can carry out several of these operations at once. Along with the scenic qualities that it shares, in its way, with theater, film's presentation includes plastic contours that it can exploit in different ways than are possible on the stage.

Particularly in those films that do not make use of it for long stretches, this sculptural potential can give rise to a striking caesura. Fassbinder's literary adaptation *Fontane Effi Briest* (West Germany, 1974) is characterized by calm, often static camerawork. Yet this form of direction is repeatedly breached in significant ways. In one passage, we see Effi (Hanna Schygulla) with her husband, Baron von Innstetten (Wolfgang Schenck), in the stairwell of a stately building, climbing a spiral staircase to their Berlin apartment. Effi is entering a world that is foreign to her; she is accompanied by her husband's mistrust. The camera lingers at the foot of the stairwell and pans to follow the path of the figures even when they can no longer be seen from below. Only the sound of their footsteps can be heard. With its low-angle perspective in the multistory building, the camera measures the social heights to which the couple is ascending. At the same time, the rotation of the gaze takes on an autonomous quality, becoming a rotation of the object of the gaze. The space itself begins to turn. An inverse vertigo effect sets in. The scene presents a negative image of the fear of heights that holds Effi (and in different way, the baron as well) prisoner.

Actors

Moreover, the ubiquitous mobility of the camera (which itself remains invisible for the most part) allows film to bring even inanimate objects into the position of subjects of its narratives. By means of a shot's composition and by means of montage, film can grant objects an entrance and an exit, a physiognomic presence and a gestural agency, in a way that would scarcely be possible in a picture or on the stage (the realization of autonomy by the thing-world at the end of *Zabriskie Point* represents a radical manifestation of film's capabilities in this regard). At the same time, the human actors in a feature film have to put up with competition from the camera; it places the actors' performances in the picture in a manner that is far from being determined solely by their physical actions at the particular site of filming. The camera not only processes; it *acts*: it offers an interpretation of whatever comes into its field of vision, in the manner in which it takes it into its visual field. To be sure, one must exercise caution when speaking of an "action of the camera." What "the camera" achieves in a film is the product of a more or less dense *composition* of its movements and its shots. It arises from the camera's connection to episodes, sequences, and ultimately to a film's higher rhythm, generated by image and sound, that inevitably influences what gets represented at a certain point or in a certain passage of any particular film.

This triad formed of literal and metaphoric actors together with the acting camera is everywhere in force in the aesthetics of the feature film. This applies, as well, to the "trick films" to which Panofsky refers in the passage cited above. In them, the boundaries between human and nonhuman actors and the willful behavior of objects and devices is fluid in any case. Walt Disney's first color film, *The Band Concert* (USA, 1935), has a veritable tornado emerge out of the background to give all the supposed subjects and objects within the filmic space a proper spin, mixing everything up thoroughly.[3] More recent, computer-generated animated films like *Shrek* (Andrew Adamson and Vicky Jenson, USA, 2001) or *Ice Age* (Chris Wedge and Carlos Saldanha, USA, 2002) also unfold in a combination of changing perspectives on fictional actors and the recalcitrant objects of their actions and inactions, figures that negotiate countless affairs with one another, brought together, often enough, by means of sophisticated image work.

But the difference between the cinema and the performing arts manifests itself with particular clarity in the disparate position of actors in film and on stage. The theater lives by the bodily movement of actors before the eyes of an audience. All performers—whether actors, dancers, extras, or even musicians—are physically present on the stage. They are present only as they appear from the particular vantage point of the observers, in their position within the domain of the performance. They interact with the audience, and in consequence their performance remains permanently bound to the moment of its realization, existing within a tension of successful and failed delivery. By contrast, the performers in a feature film act within an inaccessible and immutable virtual space that is produced by the automatic projection of image sequences. They appear there in a configuration of shifting takes in which they are presented up close or from a distance, placed in confrontation with one another in shot and reverse shot, their stances and actions cast in shifting light; each cut can conjure up a new situation, and every change of tone can alter the atmosphere. Cinema audiences are not the only ones subject to that temporal and spatial "dictate" of filmic movement discussed in chapter 2. It extends to the actors in feature films as well; their performance is dependent on the type of motion and emotion that they are permitted by the film's movement of sound and image. Of course, this in no way diminishes the accomplishment of film actors. Stage presence and screen presence are not the same, however.[4] In classical theater, the actors embody a role that is prescribed by the drama. Certainly, there is the occasional equivalent in cinema as well— Philip Marlowe embodied by Humphrey Bogart, Robert Mitchum, Elliott Gould, and James Garner, among others—but even in cases such as these, what is demanded of the actors is not really the interpretation of a prescribed role. What is demanded of them is that they *be* the particular figure, that they act in front of the camera in such a way that *their* treatment plays a major role in shaping the particular character. This also explains why the roles film actors play over the course of their career take on considerably higher significance than is the case in the theater: what is decisive with regard to their aura as performers is not their interpretation of prescribed roles, but rather their fusion with a particular character *type*.

Not only can film transform things into actors; it can turn actors into things as well. On the stage, a sleeping female figure remains physically present in the form of the performer's body; the situation is quite different in film. After a change of scene toward the end of *Fontane Effi Briest*, we see the heroine, now shunned by her husband and her parents, in the background of the image, lying on a bed asleep with her shoes on. As the camera travels slowly through the interior of the room, the furnishings partly obstruct the view of the protagonist. The camera comes to a standstill as the sleeping figure becomes partially visible again. The figure lies there like an abandoned doll. We see no breathing. She holds a letter in her hand; banknotes and sections of newspapers are strewn about the edge of the bed. The lens of the camera slips past her as if she were another element of the interior. She has become one object among others, one for whom there is no longer any place in her accustomed sphere. This verdict is delivered by a female voice that reads a letter to Effi from her mother during the traveling shot; it informs Effi in gentle diction, but with unmistakable clarity, that she has become a *persona non grata* even for her parents.

Voices

Fassbinder's *Fontane Effi Briest* is perhaps the most literary adaptation of a novel ever filmed. This lies principally in finely wrought voice direction, which allows the text of the novel to be constantly present, beyond exchanges of dialogue. The film begins with a static shot of Effi's parental home, while the reticent voice of the director reads the corresponding description from the novel. Time and again, this voice returns to comment on the state of the drama unfolding on the screen. Other female and male voices often read passages from letters that—as in the scene described above—provide a supplemental perspective on the particular sequence. The sound of these words, spoken from outside of the image events, introduces a constant counterpoint to these events. The transfer of the novel into another medium simultaneously engenders a transformed reading of its text.

At another extreme in the relative autonomization of the phenomenon of the voice vis-à-vis image movement is Alejandro González Iñárritu's eleven-minute filmic oratorio in his contribution to *11'09"01—September 11*, the anthology film produced by Alain Brigand (USA, France, 2002). For long stretches, the screen is black, and we hear a vibrating, multilingual hum of voices from which we can make out distinct news bulletins from the day of the attacks in the United States; musical rhythms are layered beneath the voices. Inserted into this acoustic collage are noises and shocked reactions from original sound recordings of the attacks on New York's Twin Towers, as well as answering machine messages left by passengers on the plane that crashed over Pennsylvania. Fragments of footage of people who jumped from the burning skyscrapers and of the towers' collapse briefly interrupt the pure black of the image. At the end of the segment, the acoustic drone is partly overlaid by elegiac orchestral music while the screen lightens to white. Here, a filmic sound installation offers an abstinent representation of the unrepresentability of horror as a response to every explanatory appropriation.[5]

This use of voices in Fassbinder and Iñárritu is far removed from classical dialogue direction in the feature film, whether it be the wordplay of the Marx Brothers films or the screwball comedies of the same period. At the end of *Bringing Up Baby* (Howard Hawks, USA, 1938), before the erotic tension between the protagonists Dr. David Huxley (Cary Grant) and Susan Vance (Katherine Hepburn) is diffused with a loud roar, there is a hilarious fifteen-minute showdown in a police station involving more and more protagonists, ultimately including two leopards. Fireworks of dialogue like this would be perfectly well suited for performance on the stage. However, the presentation would be entirely different in that setting. That is because, in cinema, actors' voices, too, are subject to a specific type of direction. They, too, can be brought in up close or from a distance, in succession or overlapping one another, from off screen or within the depicted situation, in the presence of the performers or in their absence; and all this takes place together with a calculated shifting of perspectives on the figures involved. The pictorial concentration on the faces and gestures of those who are speaking at a particular moment can—as in the sequence from *Bringing Up Baby*—facilitate a narrow focus on the facial and vocal dimensions of the performance in a way that is impossible on the spoken theater stage.

A scene at the end of *Apocalypse Now* (Francis Ford Coppola, USA, 1979) operates with an entirely different admixture of image and sound. In a parallel montage with the ritual killing of a bull, the slaughter of the murderous Colonel Walter E. Kurtz (Marlon Brando) is carried out by Captain Willard (Martin Sheen). Accepted, if not orchestrated, by the victim, the deed is barely visible in the darkness of the scene. The music that had resonated now fades. In its place, for a second, the sound of a helicopter propeller can be heard—completely unmotivated at the level of the story (it is the film's primary acoustic leitmotif). We see how Willard slowly stands up in front of an orange background and stares at the dying Kurtz. Next we see a side close-up of Kurtz's head; he is lying on the ground, and his head, illuminated in the darkness, is still moving slightly. The insane colonel utters his last words, taken from Joseph Conrad's novella *Heart of Darkness*: "The horror, the horror." As the next cut to the paralyzed Willard shows, Kurtz still exerts power over his executioner with these words, which only express the quintessence of his theory of war. The whispered sound of the two words, repeated once, is acoustically injected into the atmosphere of the preceding scenes as well as those that follow.

Theatricality

Despite all their differences, however, the cinema often forges an aesthetic alliance with the theater: not only because theater spaces have served all along as a preferred *showplace* for films; not only because cinema, too, likes to make use of a *metaphorics* of theater; but also because it has at its disposal its own forms of theatrical staging.

At the beginning of *The Searchers*, directly after the passage I described at the opening of the first chapter, there is a veritable theatrical entrance as Ethan Edwards approaches his brother's farm. In a static side shot, from the left, the camera directs its gaze at the porch of the house as, one by one, the rest of the family members step out onto it. The same staging is repeated once more at the end of the film as Ethan (along with his helper and the rescued Debbie) rides toward another farmhouse. The neighbors of the brother's family—wiped out but for Debbie—walk one by one onto the porch, seen this time from the right. The scene is set as in the theater, the first time for the coming calamity and at the end for a fragile reconciliation. The space into which the actors standing on the small stage direct their gaze is not the space of the audience, however, but the expanse of filmic space out of which Ethan Edwards rides once more near the end of the film, only to ride off into it again in the final shot.

But even in an extremely conventional orientation of the gaze, a highly unconventional assimilation of theater to the cinema is possible. In Werner Schroeter's film *Salome* (West Germany, 1971), based on Oscar Wilde's play of the same name, the camera, which is directed at the steps of an ancient ruin, remains in a single position throughout. The camera intervenes in the drama of this stage, which is never presented to the audience in a wide shot, exclusively by means of pans, zooms, and cuts, along with a collage of excerpts from the Richard Strauss opera. Lars von Trier allows himself a no less ostentatious flirtation with the theater in *Dogville* (Denmark et al., 2003), a film that is played out almost entirely on a stage set, but which moves as freely in its own space as any film—and ultimately opens this space up to a step outside that brings death. The mysterious role-plays in David Lynch's *Mulholland Drive* (USA, 2001) culminate in, among other things, an episode in a theater in which the formal possibilities of both art forms become intertwined almost to the point of indistinguishability. In *North by Northwest*, practically all of the protagonists hold one another in nearly constant suspicion of play-acting in one way or another—this, ironically, in a film that in its formal composition articulates a stark counterposition to the aesthetics of the theater. For what Hitchcock displays for his audience here is the artistic arsenal of the cinema.

In contrast, the film *To Be or Not to Be* by Ernst Lubitsch (USA, 1942) dwells by and large in the theater. Filmed in the period of the Japanese attack on Pearl Harbor and subsequent entry of the United States into the Second World War, it is at once a fast-paced screwball comedy and one of the most humane propaganda films ever made. It celebrates the stubbornness of neurotic individuals in the face of the murderous coercion of a totalitarian regime. In the guise of a satirical farce, the film enacts the world of the theater as a microcosm of all-too-human passions. Lubitsch's film mobilizes the outrageous improvisational art of a troupe of Warsaw theater people against the brutal theatrics of the German invaders. (In a related way, in his *Inglourious Basterds* [USA, 2009], Quentin Tarantino sets the grotesque adventurism of cinema against the terror of the Nazi regime.) Again and again, the patriotic deployment of the characters in *To Be or Not to Be* is torpedoed, yet at the same time spurred on, by extreme vanity, jealousy, and reckless high spirits. At the end of the film, it comes to a verbal showdown in the foyer of a theater, during a visit by Hitler, between soldiers of the German occupation and the actors, disguised as high-ranking Nazi officers. Among them is also the fake *Führer*, played by one of the supporting actors, whose disconcerting performance in the streets of Warsaw opened the film. The camera pans and tracks from guards standing in rank and file to the door of the women's restroom, out of which steps the actor Greenberg (Felix Bressart), looking disheveled. His whole life, Greenberg has dreamed in vain of playing a leading role; now, within the fiction of the film, he must play the lead in real life. As he is aggressively surrounded by the guards, his confederates— coming out of the men's restroom—walk up from behind, push themselves to the front, and call him to account. To the masklike face of the supposed *Führer*, Greenberg intones Shylock's great monologue from Shakespeare's *The Merchant of Venice*. The confusion is perfect. Once again, the actors, narcissistic and falsely pious though they may be, succeed in leading their opponents astray—and thus in doing justice to the topos of a "world turned upside down."

Attractionism

Yet the various forms in which cinema can seek out a closeness to the theater are by no means the crucial dimension of its own, inherent theatricality. Indeed, the latter requires no reference to the theater at the level of content. It proves to be another fundamental formal characteristic of the cinematic film: that it is—in a perfectly literal sense—a spectacle of its own kind.

To understand cinema as an autonomous variety not only of architecture, music, and the image, but also of the spectacle is not only a matter of perceiving its relationship with the theater and other performing arts. It entails, at the same time, recognizing the specific visual attraction of filmic processes. Films do not merely represent *something* spectacular; they represent a particular spectacle *in themselves*—and this, often enough, just when they have nothing spectacular to represent. Where films exploit this potential, they perform their spectacles for the spectators while presenting them with the spectacle of their performance. Every film discussed in this book up to now can offer an illustration. They all bear witness to an aesthetic attractionism that constitutes another fundamental dimension of this art form.

The concept of "attractionism" is borrowed from Tom Gunning's investigations into the early phase of cinema, when it was still primarily a fairground entertainment. According to the author, cinema in this period was distinguished by an "aesthetic of astonishment" that was antithetical to the "narrative cinema" that established itself as the dominant form of popular film from the time of D. W. Griffith's productions. For Gunning, the basic disposition of this "cinema of attractions" is as follows:

> Rather than being an involvement with narrative action or empathy with character psychology, the cinema of attractions solicits a highly conscious awareness of the film image engaging the viewer's curiosity. The spectator does not get lost in a fictional world and its drama, but remains aware of the act of looking, the excitement of curiosity and its fulfilment.[6]

One can take up this observation and make systematic use of it once the all-too-linear historical thesis of an evolution of film from a pole of attraction to a pole of narration has been submitted to a vigorous correction. After all, as regards the evolution of film since Griffith, it would be difficult to discount the fact that both poles have always been in force within cinema and have remained in force to the present day.[7] With that, of course, the opposition between a cinema of "narration" and a cinema of "astonishment" dissolves—and it becomes possible to take seriously the particular visual attraction of cinema, without reservations with regard to its narrative, imaginative, and immersive power.

A primary, simple form of filmic attractionism consists in the fact that something highly astounding is happening on the screen. In *A Night at the Opera*, there is an episode of around seven minutes that remains bound to the early cinema of spectacle. On a luxury liner, Otis B. Driftwood (Groucho) has been assigned to a tiny cabin, just big enough for the bed and his enormous trunk. Enter the three stowaways Tomasso (Harpo), Fiorello (Chico), and the tenor Riccardo Baroni (Allan Jones)—and suddenly the room is somewhat overcrowded. Now the camera watches, in a mainly static take, as the cabin fills up with more and more people. In come two chambermaids, a ship's engineer and his assistant, a manicurist, and a young woman who just wants to make a quick phone call. Despite the rather dire predicament (and as far as the women are concerned, molestation by Harpo), they all go about their business, undaunted. Finally, four waiters come in carrying big silver trays on their shoulders, and the hungry Harpo leaps on the food with a belly flop. As it happens, however, Groucho had scheduled a rendezvous with Mrs. Claypool (Margaret Dumont) for just this time. When she opens the cabin door, the whole throng comes tumbling out with aplomb, landing indelicately at the feet of this respectable personage, to her great dismay.

It is no accident that the films of the Marx Brothers are often structured as multiact revues that form a more or less unified whole. Many action and disaster films follow the same principle. In *Independence Day* (Roland Emmerich, USA, 1996), there is a sequence in which skyscrapers in large American cities are reduced to cinders, one by one, by hostile aliens in giant UFOs using some sort of laser beam. In *True Lies* (James Cameron, USA, 1994), Harry Tasker (Arnold Schwarzenegger) pursues a terrorist, who is fleeing on a motorcycle, on horseback, riding a police horse through a luxury hotel (much to the consternation of the guests and personnel). He guides his mount into a glass elevator, rides up an exterior shaft to the roof of the hotel, where he tries to coax the animal into making a giant leap over the street canyon below; the horse sensibly refuses, creating a comic resolution to the dramatic scene. Martial arts cinema constitutes a special variant, in which the continuity of the story is interrupted periodically by the dance of artistic, gravity-defying combat—one thinks of the *Matrix* trilogy (Larry and Andy Wachowski, USA, 1999–2003) or *Hero* (*Ying xiong*) by Zhang Yimou (China, 2002). A film like *Avatar* (James Cameron, USA, 2009) combines these methods with the spectacular visual effects of computer-animated 3D cinema.

This episodic quality is not necessarily related to the second, formal aspect of filmic attractionism, although the latter can always combine with the former. This second aspect derives its fascination from an astonishing *way of staging* film scenes and scene sequences; this is completely independent of whether and to what extent these scenes have a spectacular, sensational, or otherwise intense character in themselves. Here it is not what is presented, but the presentation that is able to capture our attention. The anarchy of perspectives in the final sequence of *A Night at the Opera* is an example; likewise the race through Moscow, composed of chords of color and rhythm, in *The Bourne Supremacy*. Another, certainly, is the montage of real-time and slow-motion shots at the end of *Zabriskie Point*, which bring forth in the image the dance-like action of objects detached from their utilitarian function. How the events *in* the film are evoked or formed or colored by the event *of* the film: this is what constitutes the particular formal attraction of the filmic moving image.

Certainly one can watch any one of the above films without paying much attention to the formal qualities from which its intensity arises. But these qualities are there. They are visible. They not only contribute to the film's development; they often sustain it. Precisely in films that draw their visual attraction from episodes of excessive or extravagant action, the suspense of the events on the screen arises from the linkage of content-related and formal aspects. Here too, what happens is contingent on how the film manifests what happens in its audiovisual composition. With these films too, our enjoyment of them does not solely depend on the way in which they are staged, and in any case, their enjoyment is perfectly compatible with an awareness of their formal operations. As with the perception of artistic images, a "twofold attention" to these films is always possible and, indeed, always necessary for a full appreciation of their aesthetic composition.

Ecstasy

There are films in which one would take no interest whatsoever if one did not allow oneself to be caught up in their movement of sound and image. Wong Kar-Wai's film *In the Mood for Love* (*Fa yeung nin wa*; Hong Kong, France, Thailand, 2000) is about the love between a man and a woman,

both betrayed by their respective spouses, who renounce the physical consummation of their passion. The ascetic commitment that binds Li-zhen
Chan (Maggie Cheung) und Chow Mo-wan (Tony Leung) to one another
is made visible on the screen by a directorial approach that keeps a resolute distance from the characters; it dramatizes the distance that the lovers
maintain from each other. The camera never plunges into situations that
are shared by the couple. Instead, again and again, it moves alongside the
spaces in which they are together in their restrained intimacy, confining itself to observing from the outside the interiors where the couple lingers.
The film places its own gestures before those of the actors, fostering an atmosphere of erotic melancholy.

In one sequence, we see Mrs. Chan through an open door, sitting on a
stool, alone in her rented room. A kitschy song is playing on the radio that
her husband, who is away on a business trip, gave to her as a birthday gift.
In the background, we see a kitchen cupboard and on the counter next to
it, at the edge of the image, a small kettle from which steam is escaping—
a casual metaphor for sexual heat. The camera moves to the left in the
direction of the neighboring room, which is occupied by Mr. Chow. The
camera's gaze is interrupted by the wall that separates the apartments, and
the image goes black before opening up again to reveal, in one-third of the
screen, a view of the young man, sitting in a chair reading. As the song is
heard again, the camera pauses briefly, then moves slowly back to the shot
of Li-zhen, who is likewise framed in black by the walls of the hallway,
and lingers there for several seconds. A telephone rings. Cut. As the music
goes silent and the sounds of an office are heard in the background, the
camera again moves along a wall, coming to a stop at the close-up of a
telephone. Cut. We see half of a large wall clock. We hear the voice of
Mo-wan over the telephone, who asks Li-zhen, in a moment of tempta-
tion, if they should leave the city of Hong Kong. Cut. Again, the camera
travels along a wall; with its black, gold, and red elements, it creates the
effect of an abstract painting, though it is recognizable to the audience as
part of the hotel in which the lovers have sometimes met. A tango song,
which has no localized source in the scene, is heard during this tracking
shot. When the camera stops, we see Mo-wan, ready to go out, standing
in a contemplative pose in a doorway that creates a golden frame, next to
which hangs a red curtain. He turns, moves into the interior of the room,
and turns off the light. With that, the image goes mostly black again, lit

only by two gold vertical stripes and one red one, as if one were standing in front of a picture by Barnett Newman. As happens so often in this film, the filmic space in which Li-zhen and Mo-wan might have encountered one another without inhibitions transforms into a space of images whose ardor replaces the couple's deferred pleasure. The characters in the film are not alone in living out their desire in the ecstasy of abstinence; the film itself persists in an attitude of passionate renunciation.

5

FILM AS NARRATIVE

Three Films

The seventy-four-minute film *Five—Dedicated to Yasujiro Ozu* by Abbas Kiarostami (Iran, 2003) consists of five long, static takes. The first is directed toward a seashore, where the water is toying with two washed-up pieces of wood. The second shows a seaside boardwalk with passersby walking to and fro. In the third, we see dogs encamped on the beach as the brightness of the light changes and the horizon grows increasingly diffuse. The fourth presents the play of light in reverse, with the gaze once again directed toward a shore. Ducks file past in a row, first intermittently from left to right, then in a large troop from right to left. In the transition to the last and by far the longest take, strains of a zither and an accordion come in as the screen goes black. Then we hear dogs barking, the croaking of frogs, and the sounds of other animals. Accompanied by the ebbing and flowing music of these sounds, moonlight becomes visible on a surface of water, its reflection growing now larger, now smaller.

Later, thunderclaps and the rush of rain become audible; lightning produces flickering images for fractions of a second. After this, the screen goes dark again for a while, until unseen clouds disperse. The moon resumes its painting on the water, and the animals give voice again. At the end, the crowing of a rooster announces the dawn. In the last minute and a half, the screen becomes increasingly bright, revealing a view of a gently rippling surface of water.

Although everything in this last episode appears as if it were filmed in a single, continuous take, this is by no means the case. Even the comic spectacle of the parade of ducks on the shore is indebted to sophisticated staging. This film's apparent artlessness is the product of thoroughly artful composition. The contemplative gaze that it enables has as its source a highly concentrated filmic seeing and hearing. Herein lies the homage to the work of Japanese director Ozu. In contrast to Ozu's feature films, however, in *Five* absolutely nothing is narrated. Kiarostami's film lingers on views that neither contain elements of a story nor add up to fragments of a story. In the absence of narrative progression, observers are subjected to a phenomenal abundance of appearing that is present particularly where relatively little is happening. The film brings into presence the individuality and thus the incomprehensibility of the real, including that of the filmic image itself.

The documentary short film *Mülheim (Ruhr)* by Peter Nestler and Reinald Schnell (West Germany, 1964) follows a related aesthetic principle. This ten-minute symphony of a small city takes the form of a revue composed of predominantly static, black-and-white images. In a montage buttressed by the austere sounds of a guitar and a Jew's harp, it sketches a highly contrasting portrait of a city, accompanied neither by original sounds nor by verbal commentary. Destruction and rebuilding, past and future, work world and leisure time, everyday life and celebrations, are illuminated in rhythmic variations. Moods of bleakness and expectation alternate on the screen. The physiognomies of buildings and people are registered with equanimous intensity. The film explores the interior landscape of this city without proposing a conclusive image of it. The many fleeting situations, contemporary at the time, that are captured in these images coalesce into an archaeology of historical time. Depending on the age of today's viewer, the sunken world of this city will appear in a varying mixture of familiarity and strangeness. Correspondences stand out that could hardly have been as perceptible in the year of this film's production. The pictorial worlds of de Chirico and Cartier-Bresson shine through, but so too do those of Bernd and Hilla Becher, whose photographic investigations of the industrial architecture of the day were just coming into being at the time. In the photos taken in pubs, we see faces that call Romy Schneider or Fritz Walter to mind. Yet these are reminiscences that the film evokes precisely because it refrains, in its perception, from further interpretation. It remains open to the heterogeneity of the views it has captured. It moves within a landscape that is full of the traces of collective and individual history, yet it picks up none of these threads. It leads its viewers into a space of possible narratives, but it does not even allude to following through with a single one.

Romuald Karmakar's *Hamburger Lektionen* (Germany, 2006) offers another example of cinema's refusal with regard to narrative. After minimalistic opening credits, we see, across a wide roadway, a nondescript row of houses in the Hamburg district of St. Georg. This spare shot lasts fifteen seconds. It will remain the only outdoor shot in the entire film, which runs over two hours. The screen goes black. A few lines of text give information about the life of the Salafi preacher Mohammed Ben Mohammed al-Fazazi, who was the imam of the Al-Quds Mosque in Hamburg for several years until October 2001. The mosque is located in an office building, which is seen in the film's initial shot. The film's closing credits will convey the supplemental information that three of the 9/11 hijackers had close contact with Fazazi and regularly attended his sermons. On January 3 and 5, 2000, the last days of Ramadan, it is explained, Fazazi held so-called lessons (*Lektionen*). These were recorded on video by an unknown person and distributed in various bookstores. "Their exact wording is reproduced here in full." The introduction ends with this statement. Again the screen goes black.

Reproduce the *exact wording* of these teachings: Karmakar's film follows this stage direction with extraordinary precision. After the date and time of the first lesson is faded in, we see the actor Manfred Zapatka sitting in a studio in front of a dark background, wearing reading glasses and dressed in everyday clothes. He holds manuscript pages in his hand and reads from them. The reading extends throughout the film until, at the end, Zapatka stands up and leaves the room. The shot of the reader alternates between side and frontal views, during which Zapatka often looks directly into the camera. To the left and right of the actor are two small tables. He places pages from the manuscript on one, and from the other he takes new ones. Sometimes a hand passes him additional pages from beyond the boundary of the screen. Otherwise nothing happens. In a sober and focused tone, Zapatka reproduces the preacher's speeches. Terms that would require explanation for a non-Muslim audience are explained in a slightly different vocal inflection. Even occasional background noises (audible on the video), interjections, and questions from the audience are placed on record by Zapatka. All that can be heard is the actor's reciting voice. He delivers the transcript of Fazazi's statements without even tentatively embodying him. Performer and performance reject any mimesis, any masquerade, any commentary—and any embellishing narrative. Zapatka's extremely reticent facial expressions and the absence of gesture produce a considerable estrangement effect. The words spoken by the preacher are presented verbatim. In a *gestus* of negative theatricality, the film draws its suspense from the progression of the imam's messages—at first seemingly rather harmless, then veiled, and finally openly fanatical. In its radical focus on the mounting monstrosity of what is being said, the film stages a renunciation of staging.

Abstinence

Abstinence is possible. There are nonnarrative cinematic films, films that, as they run their course, forgo the formation of a story. Even if they contain traces, indications, or elements of conceivable stories, even if they provide their spectators with stimuli for imagining stories, and even if the audience knows many stories that link to the situations that are being presented, these films themselves allow no narrative to arise. Iñárritu's requiem for the terror victims of 9/11, considered in the previous chapter, is composed in this way. In chapter 2, the final sequences in Antonioni's films *L'Eclisse* and *Zabriskie Point* provided examples of ways in which feature films can opt out of their own narratives. Moreover, my interpretation of the car chase in *The Bourne Supremacy* in that same chapter demonstrated how, at their culmination points, action films frequently take a "time-out" from the furtherance of their narrative. Even in a narrative film, not every scene follows the laws of narration. Certainly, the last three films presented above suggest the degree to which the cinema can remain abstinent with regard to the praxis of narrative.

Such renunciation must be understood correctly, however. Of course, one can narrate the course of events in films like *Five*, *Mülheim (Ruhr)*, and *Hamburger Lektionen*, as I have done, in part, above. The fact that one can tell a story *about something* by no means implies that it is a story *itself*. Much that occurs in one way or another can be described in a narrative fashion without ascribing a narrative structure to the respective events. Not everything, by far, that has a chronological order has the chronological order of a narrative. This is true not only outside of the arts, but also within them. Many forms of architecture, music, modern dance, or abstract painting—and, as we have seen, some forms of cinema—have no narrative organization, although their organization can be analyzed by narrative means. Yet in only a few art forms does the renunciation of narrative take the spectacular form of an aesthetic abjuration.

Films like *Five* and *Hamburger Lektionen* that entirely forgo the development of a story reject cinema's narrative possibilities along with the corresponding conventions. These two examples make this move as feature films on the fringes of that overarching genre. *Mülheim (Ruhr)*, on the other hand, clearly belongs to documentary cinema, though this film, too, behaves in a conspicuously abstentious manner with regard to the typical narrative components of its genre. The question of the feature film's relationship to the full spectrum of filmic genres will be taken up in detail in the next chapter. For the moment, what is at issue is the affair of the feature film, in particular, with narration. As these initial examples have shown, this affair can be interrupted, but it can be broken off decisively as well. As the investigations of the previous chapters have laid out, film can certainly be understood, from an aesthetic point of view, "as" architecture, music, image, and spectacle; it cannot, without qualification, be comprehended "as narrative." Yet film has a particular narrative potential at its disposal, as nearly all of the films we have considered up to now have illustrated in their own way. The small number of films that spurn this potential leave one of cinema's genuine possibilities unused out of artistic calculation.

In this sense, the nonnarrative film represents a borderline case. Against the backdrop of an overwhelming tally of narrative films, it embodies a negative form of cinema that precisely for this reason can exert a particular attraction for its spectators, just as in the case of post-dramatic theater and forms of modern dance that have left narrative behind. Narrative literature itself is capable not only of interrupting, impeding, or protracting narration, but of suspending it nearly completely. This is what happens in Rolf Dieter Brinkmann's story *Weißes Geschirr* [White Crockery] or at the beginning of Claude Simon's novel *The Georgics* (*Les Géorgiques*). Here, too, however, this borderline case is merely the flip side of an extraordinary narrative disposition that these two art forms share.

Narrative Disposition

As far as cinema is concerned, this disposition has been under discussion throughout the first four chapters of this book. The examination of the formal composition of the filmic moving image has been at the same time a survey of the fundamental possibilities of filmic storytelling. Films' particular temporal structure makes possible a particular way of representing series of events. Their characteristic spatial structure enables films, in a way that is particular to them, to play out in the midst of the narrated action. Their distinctive auditory structure allows films to shape the situations that they present in a particular way and connect them to the situation of the audience. This constitution distinguishes film in a fundamental way from the narrative operations of literature. Films are individual configurations of image and sound movement; literature consists in individual configurations of words and sentences. Rhythm and sound play a significant role in both art forms. Yet the reading of literature is not subject to anything approaching the "temporal dictate," analyzed in the second chapter, that shapes the viewing of films in the cinema. Readers can pause, linger, reread, page ahead, digress from the text, and interrupt their reading however they like.

A divergent form of artistic imagination constitutes one flashpoint of these differences between film and literature. Certainly, literature's stories also develop an articulated imagination of the time and space in which they are set; yet a much more extensive filling in of "gaps" in the respective narrative is possible for—and also demanded of—readers of literature.[1] The literary text is a musical score performed by its readers.

By contrast, the film shown in the cinema is a presentation that binds its viewers in a far more forceful manner to its own order of events. Although the spectators in the cinema also must supplement the audio-visual action by a great deal, here their primary task is to keep up with the course of things. Films are not musical scores. They are presentations to which the audience is subjected. To follow them requires a readiness to give oneself up to them.

A special aptitude for narrative is certainly not the sole privilege of literature and cinema. Almost all the arts have an affinity for storytelling forms. Traditional theater proceeds in a narrative fashion, to be sure, but the visual arts have their own forms of narration as well. Even apart from the special characteristics of picture series mentioned in chapter 3, individual images can present a story. Paintings like *A Country Brawl* or *The Seven Acts of Mercy* by Pieter Brueghel the Younger represent a temporal before and after within their simultaneous image space. Wherever music is linked to text and scenic performance—in ballads and popular songs, but above all in opera's dramatic offerings—it too becomes a genuine medium of storytelling. Even architecture, which—unlike sculpture—has no narrative potential of its own, can enter into a liaison with the narrative arts by decorating surfaces with frescoes, by mural painting, and by the assimilation of other pictorial forms.

The narrative affinity of so many art forms is not by chance. It has its origins in the narrative disposition of human beings. Acting beings are by nature storytelling beings. They are reliant on cultures of narration. In almost every domain of life, they seek common understanding through their own stories and those of others. The art of storytelling extends far beyond the sphere of the aesthetic arts. Storytelling is an anthropologically grounded, universal practice for which the production and assimilation of artistic narratives represent a continuation as well as a break.

Telling Stories

Through stories, human beings make sense, for themselves and others, of what has happened in history and in the near-term present or what might happen in the future. They create relationships between situations and events, they elucidate how and why particular incidents and particular types of changes have come about—or could have come about. Stories address how individuals or collectives have fared or how something has played out—whether it be everyday activities, political upheavals, scientific discoveries, or processes of natural evolution. With varying degrees of complexity, stories put factual and fictional processes into a more or less comprehensibly structured context. Causal relationships always play a key role; stories reconstruct or imagine which situations and incidents were the cause of which other events. Also among a story's essential factors are the attitudes—affective and rational—of those who are or have been touched by the respective events. Ultimately, human deeds and human fates (or those of mythical figures of all sorts in which the human is reflected) are in the foreground in most everyday stories as well as artistic ones. In the context of external effective forces, stories present sentiments, moods, feelings, convictions, and intentions as they influence the behavior of the respective protagonists. The course of the recounted story arises out of these entanglements. It often moves from some significant point of departure toward a striking end point: the resolution of a conflict, a calamitous outcome, or the chiaroscuro of an open ending. Whether a story recounts the success or failure—or the success *and* failure—of actions, endeavors, projects, ambitions, and hopes, it always culminates in a bringing into presence of the particular significance that the recounted events held, hold, or could have held for those involved.

Stories can play out along the many gradations of the realis and irrealis moods. When human or humanlike actors are involved, stories nearly always recount how it is, how it was, how it would have been, or how it would be to experience the situation or suffer the fate in question. Especially when the unexpected, the unpredictable, or sheer chance is in play, and all the more when an event arises that explodes the coordinates of individuals' or collectives' previous comprehension and behavior, stories can make the causal and motivational interconnections among a number of occurrences comprehensible—or at least they can attempt to do so. In so doing, they offer explanations of how events that follow one *after* the other could or had to follow one *from* the other.

Storytelling provides an entirely different kind of insight than nomological explanation, in which that which appears, contingently, is traced back to law-like processes. As Michael Hampe writes, stories open up distinctive options for making changes visible and potentially understandable.

The story, too, masters contingency by embedding the unique and the singular within a context, yet they do not, in the process, become instances of something general, but are rather linked to *other singularities*. . . . In that sense, the story is also a type of explanation, but not one that traces the new back to the old or the different to the always-the-same; instead, it guides attention by means of precise description, so that larger contexts, transitions, plausbilities, arise that do not have to serve as the transitions of deductive conclusions.[2]

Stories, in other words, specialize in a representation of the individuality of biographical and historical processes that avoids a law-like reconstruction.

Certainly, the actual or merely apparent "contingency" of what occurs within the format of the narrative is not always, and in fact often is not, "mastered" in every respect. Randomness and chaos do not have to be banished, overcome, or eliminated in the course of a story; they can also be elaborated and exposed. Particularly in artistic stories, it is not unusual for developments to be made present precisely in their contingency, such as in Heinrich von Kleist's stories "The Earthquake in Chile" and "Michael Kohlhaas" or in the depiction of battle scenes in Claude Simon's novel *The Flanders Road* (*La Route des Flandres*). Moreover, a story's focus on the particularity of an event constellation does not contradict a possible universality of its content. In the form of an exemplary representation, stories can allow the general contours of a situation, a conflict, or a fate to emerge from an individual incident.

The standpoint from which the particular events are reported can also have exemplary significance. Every story, through the manner of its composition, presents a way of seeing whatever it presents. At the same time, with processes that are specific to them, stories construct specific forms of commentary and also of justification. As regards the legitimation, delegitimation, or other types of valuation of individual or collective action, stories can communicate the normative attitudes from which those actions originate more forcefully than other forms of commentary and justification. What is more, they can connect this with the formation of an evaluative stance toward the depicted events and perspectives. This manifests itself not so much through explicit valuation, but primarily in the style of the narration in question. Stories that proceed in this way lend a distinct intensification not only to what is recounted, but also to the story itself.

They make understandable or put in question the degree to which actions in a given situation are appropriate or inappropriate, just or unjust,
measured or crazy; they clarify the quotient of justice or injustice, rea-
sonableness or unreasonableness, likely or improbable circumstances, the
astounding or the banal, that has befallen the active or passive participant.
Through the *how* of storytelling—in the choice of words, the selection
of scenes, the composition of the beginning and ending, by lingering on
particular events and overlooking others, by drawing out or accelerating
the course of action, and by many other stylistic means—stories cast a
specific light, colored in one way or another by valuation, on the *what*
of the events presented. Every story inevitably gives an interpretation of
what it recounts.

Perspectivity

This perspectivity of narration has a distinguishing trait. The viewpoints
that stories open up on the actions and suffering, the opinions and striv-
ing, of their characters are never entirely congruent with the perspective
of the agents in the story. To a greater or lesser degree, the perspective *on*
the characters differs from the perspective *of* the characters. Peter Goldie
has aptly commented on this constitutive tension within narrative discourse: "The interplay between diverging perspectives in a narrative—
between internal and evaluative, as well as in the evaluative domain—is
one of the main sources of its power as a medium of thought in explaining and expressing what it is to lead a life as a person."[3] To lead life as a
person includes the ability simultaneously to distinguish one's own perspectives from those of others and to place these perspectives in relation
to one another, as occurs in paradigmatic fashion in the story format.
Stories and storytellers have no choice but to offer perspectives on the
recounted events that, because they are *narrative* perspectives, diverge
more or less widely from the viewpoints of the characters that the story is
about. The primary reason for this is that the perspective of a story differs
with regard to chronology from that of the actors in the story. This temporal distance is accompanied by asymmetries of knowledge and judgment with regard to the situations and events that the bonds of the story
hold together. In this way, tension arises between the standpoint of the

story with regard to the situations in which its protagonists move, on one hand, and on the other, with regard to the standpoint of the protagonists, from which they negotiate the respective situations. Goldie subsumes this relationship under the concept of "dramatic irony." Here this term does not stand for a particular style of narration, but rather for the fundamental divergence between the perspective (or perspectives) *of* an event made present in a narrative and the perspective (or perspectives) *within* this event. "The very fact of dramatic irony shows that imagining the perspectives of those who are internal to the narrative is not sufficient for narrative appreciation."[4]

Although the concept of dramatic irony is borrowed from the theory of the theater, it underscores a general characteristic of narrative.

> The point applies not only to fictional narratives, but to works of history, to autobiographies, to diaries and contemporary historical documents, and to confessions. All these kinds of narratives, when concerned with people, have this special explanatory, revelatory, and expressive power, which can remind us of, and throw light on, the subtle and complex ways in which perspectives can diverge.[5]

Admittedly, this divergence appears with varying degrees of overtness in different forms and variants of narrative; it may remain more subliminal or become prominent. It is always present, however, as a self-evident ingredient of narrative communication and self-understanding, even if in the everyday practice of storytelling it often remains unnoticed. It is primarily in the domain of artistic representation that this internal imbalance of narrative is dramatized with particular salience and complexity. The narrative arts frequently employ a diversity of conflicting perspectives, making the internal tension of narrative into a focal point of their organization. They play with this potential and exploit it.

Here we come across an additional facet of that twofold attention that is also required in the perception of artistic images. It touches on the duality of movement *in* film and *of* film, considered in chapter 2, as well as the polarity between "attraction" and "narration" within filmic presentation, analyzed in the preceding chapter. Certainly, the tension that is now our focus is emblematic of all the arts that proceed in a narrative fashion. Even putting aside for a moment the tangle of perspectives in a novel like Marcel Proust's *In Search of Lost Time* or, as concerns cinema, films like Robert Altman's *Short Cuts* (USA, 1993) or Rainer Werner Fassbinder's *Berlin Alexanderplatz* (West Germany, 1980), every narrative feature film gives rise to friction between incongruent perspectives. John Ford's *The Searchers* presents its hero Ethan Edwards in his self-image as a supremely competent Westerner who will never let himself be dominated by anyone or anything, but at the same time as a wanderer driven by highly dubious impulses. Alfred Hitchcock's *North by Northwest* leads its characters, over and over again, into situations in which they suspect each other of hiding their true identities. The film also leaves the viewers uncertain about the true nature of the characters' actions and attitudes. At the beginning of the story, the viewers know only that enemy agents have mistaken Roger Thornhill for a certain George Kaplan. But they have no more clue than most of the film's other characters that this figure is an inner-fictional invention of an American intelligence agency. The successive revelation of this fiction entails a relativization of the perspectives of almost every character involved. This game of perspectives loses nothing of its perfidiousness with multiple viewings of the film. On the contrary, such repetition tends to enhance it, since now the ironies of the narrative can be savored from the beginning with open eyes.

Filmic Storytelling

Contrasts of the type described above occur even in everyday narratives— but they are present all the more in the form of religious, historical, and political grand narratives, and those of myth and art as well. In these domains, too, film brings its characteristic possibilities into play. Even more than other narrative forms, film can unfold from the inside out the situations through which it moves, because everything that becomes visible and audible in the course of a film is realized within a horizon of spaces and times that remain detached from the events on the big screen or the small one. In this way, film is capable of guiding the perception of its viewers in and through a virtual world that can only be experienced by seeing and hearing—into a world, to be sure, that is akin to the real one to a widely variable degree and that can be referred to the real world to an equally variable extent. This disposition enables narrative cinema to present situations with extraordinary intensity from the standpoint of the participants in those situations and, at the same time, to open up a view of the larger contexts in which the depicted actions and fates take place, thereby acquainting the audience with a perspective that differs to a greater or lesser degree from that of the characters taking these actions. This is one of the reasons that, especially in significant feature films, the events they dramatize are made clear, only to be rendered enigmatic again—just as always happens in the great artistic stories.

Through to the end of *The Searchers*, it remains obscure what motivates Ethan Edwards—a man whose previous life, after fighting on the side of the South in the American Civil War, remains largely in the shadows—to search for years for his abducted niece Debbie. After he declares multiple times that the young woman's life is no longer worth living, what brings him to clasp her in his arms and take her "home" is all the more mysterious. *Taste of Cherry* by Abbas Kiarostami traces what might be the last day in the life of a man who intends to take his own life, without providing the slightest indication of his reasons. The hero of *The Bourne Supremacy* by Paul Greengrass knows as little as the viewers following him in his violent search how he came be who he is. Only fragments of his past become discernible, little by little, to him and to the audience (fragments that are pieced together in part in *The Bourne Ultimatum* [Paul Greengrass, USA, 2007]). Each of these films is centered around its main characters to a large degree; they are present on the screen over long stretches. But they are ushered through a space of filmic occurrence that is incomprehensible both for these figures and for the viewers—so that not only the characters' horizon, but also that of the audience is being perpetually transcended.

Literature, to be sure, has other means of representing its characters' sensitivities. Young Werther and the Young Törless, Wilhelm Meister and Anna Karenina, the Idiot and the Unnamable, Mrs. Dalloway and Professor Pnin, to name just a few characters that lend their names to the novels in which they appear, are all given shape by virtue of their intellectual disposition and their inner lives being brought into presence, to a degree that film can seldom reach. The internal monologue of Lieutenant Gustl in Arthur Schnitzler's story of the same name or that of Molly Bloom in the final chapter of James Joyce's *Ulysses* lets loose a stream of consciousness that advances like filmic movement, but it could never be translated into the language of film.

Here, once again, we see a countervailing tendency in the disposition of the two art forms. It concerns the relationship between situation and experiencing in the characterization of the respective figures in film and literature. The feature film gives primacy to the representation of the situation in which the protagonists' actions are carried out over these characters' experiencing—even and precisely when what is being represented is their experiencing. For the most part, film shows that its characters are moved internally by bringing into presence the situations through which they move. Literature, by contrast, gives primacy to the representation of subjects' experiencing over the situations in which they find themselves—even and precisely when what is being represented are these situations. It can more powerfully portray the motive force of the situations through which their characters travel from the perspective of the emotion that seizes them in these situations.

This countervailing tendency must not be understood as a strict opposition, however. Narrative films and works of narrative literature can give way to the divergence of the basic orientation of their media to varying degrees—indeed, they can disavow this divergence altogether. Fassbinder's *Fontane Effi Briest* neutralizes the opposition between literary and cinematographic characterization in a highly sophisticated manner. The film *Blue* by Derek Jarman (Great Britain, 1993) forgoes bringing specific situations visually into presence. Apart from the opening and closing credits, we see nothing but a blue screen throughout the course of the film. The tale of woe is recounted in fragments, conveyed entirely by a montage of voices. In the novel *Jealousy* (*La Jalousie*) by Alain Robbe-Grillet, an atmosphere of jealousy arises through a description of external circumstances that withholds any direct representation of subjective emotions.

Yet it is in the differences of degree between the techniques of literature and film that the structural difference in the two art forms' temporality makes itself apparent. The deviation in the way they guide their respective recipients entails at the same time a divergence in the very process of executing narration. Stories are not only developed differently in literature and film; they also play out differently. By virtue of its material constitution as the reproduction of an audiovisual process fixed on storage media, film irrevocably presents not only the duration of what is being narrated, but the duration of its narration as well. Film itself *is* an irreversible series of events; it *is* a continuous, causal occurrence to which the audience is subjected during its presentation in the cinema. For this reason as well, film is predestined to a particular way of presenting stories. Its pure progression dramatizes the irreversible course of history and of the stories within which agents have always moved—and it does this even when a film, in its own progression, allows itself a reversal of temporal order, as occurs in a passage of *Funny Games* (Michael Haneke, Austria, 1997) or throughout in *Memento* (Christopher Nolan, USA, 2000).

Cinema's Temporal Form

The particular continuous form of filmic narration gives rise to the particular temporal form of the stories that films tell. By virtue of the fact that viewers are inescapably subjected, in the darkness of the cinema, to whatever happens in films, everything that plays out there remains dependent on the here and now of its audiovisual appearing, including the invisible and inaudible aspects that always surround the latter. In the cinema, viewers are involved, in a singular fashion, in the *narrative* because they are involved in the *narration* in a particular way (that is to say, they are enveloped in it and bound to the course that it takes). They are situated in the present tense of an audiovisual appearing that colors everything presented in the cinema within narrative orders of a temporal and causal sequence. As our examination of the image analysis performed in *Blow-Up* has revealed, photography and film differ not least according to their temporal form. Especially for the feature film, this holds true: the tense of filmic narration is the present—even and precisely when what is being recounted lies in the distant past or future.[6]

In most narrative modes, conversely, what is recounted is irrevocably past at the moment of its narration. This is because, as participants in historical life, living beings that exercise agency move within a temporal horizon that extends beyond their present. "To exist historically is to perceive the events one lives through as part of a story later to be told," notes Arthur Danto, laconically, in his analysis of the grammar of historical narratives.[7] "The cognitive openness of the future is required if we are to believe that the shape of the future is in any way a matter of what we choose to do."[8] Human agency is only present where there is a constellation of limitless possibilities whose significance for one's own deeds and their consequences is not fixed in advance. The operations and processes of individual or collective behavior can only be cast ex post in the form of narrative explanation and interpretation. Not even filmic storytelling can render these conditions categorically inoperative. Its stories, too, are marked by the temporal and cognitive asymmetries of narrating communication. No differently than most artistic fictions (insofar as these are not open to improvisational performance, as may be the case on the stage), film's stories, too, are closed, no matter how open their endings might be. They, too, take their course by closing off their characters' options step by step. In representing what befalls their characters, they, too, move steadily toward a future that is already past. But in its manner of telling a story, cinema relates to passing time differently than the other narrative arts can do. Everything that plays out here plays out in a mode of the present-made-present.

By contrast, the predominant mode of literary narration is the preterite tense. Its fictional stories unfold according to how the destiny of its characters came to pass. Yet literature can also deviate from this model. Novels like *The Georgics (Les Géorgiques)* by Claude Simon or *The Waves* by Virginia Woolf are realized in alternating past and present tenses; others like Simon's *Leçon des Choses* [Lesson in Things], Samuel Beckett's *The Unnamable (L'Innommable)*, Alain Robbe-Grillet's *Jealousy (La Jalousie)*, or Peter Handke's *Der Hausierer* [The Peddler] are in the present tense throughout. Narrative literature can play with the dimensions of biographical and historical time, with the probable and the improbable, with the fusion of imagination and memory, in ways that historiography, duty-bound to the truth of its statements, must disavow.

With regard to this insubordinate quality of narrative, literature and cinema are clearly on the same side as the other narrative arts. As *arts*, they can take liberties that would be inappropriate or impermissible within other narrative practices. The disparity between the temporal forms of literature and cinema cannot lie in these processes, then. The difference lies, instead, in the particular present tense of filmic events themselves. Here, in cinema, what is narrated is tightly interwoven with the time of the narration. *The time* occurs as the film occurs. Film incorporates its audience into this time of its own. The stories that it tells are realized within this time of its own.

There is a crucial difference with regard to the performing arts as well. To be sure, their performances also take place in the present tense, before the eyes of an audience that is present in the same space. This is the case even and precisely in the staging of historical dramas. In this respect, film and the theater share a temporal mode. Yet by virtue of their processing space, the presences of a cinematographic presentation have a different constitution than those of a theatrical performance. An occurring space happens while the film is happening. Film takes its audience along into this space of its own. The stories that film tells are realized in this space of its own. In this way, the presentism of the cinema ultimately distinguishes itself from the live broadcasts of television and other filmic image conduits that also exhibit a pronounced present-ness. Here too, we have to do with forms of a more or less elaborate staging of sound and image; but the meaning of this staging is entirely different than in cinema. In television's live broadcasts, whether they be talk shows, airings of political events, public exhibitions, sporting events, or opera performances, it is primarily the events, taking place there and now, that are presented in a present-tense mode. Conversely, in film it is the *representation* unfolding here and now that is realized in the present tense.[9]

The Present Past

With all of the differentiations we have just made, we certainly must not forget one thing: all forms of artistic representation are distinguished by a particular present-ness. Self-presentation is a principle of all the arts, regardless of whether and to what degree they proceed along narrative lines. They present whatever they present in the constellations of their works. It is only in pursuing their inner processuality that are they perceived as artistic objects. Their aesthetic reference to the world, to the extent that they have one, arises from their aesthetic self-reference: from the configurations of their spatial, tonal, pictorial, gestural, or linguistic appearing. Every art form and every successful artwork realizes this, each in its own way. The particular temporal form even and precisely of narrative cinema is just one among many ways in which the arts create *a* particular present in *their* present.[10]

What this special cinematic time is all about is evident not least when films present stories from past times—one thinks of *The Searchers*, *The Man Who Shot Liberty Valance*, *Once Upon a Time in the West* (Sergio Leone, Italy, USA, 1968), *Barry Lyndon* (Stanley Kubrick, UK, 1975), or *Gladiator* (Ridley Scott, UK, USA, 2000). For the duration of films such as these, viewers can dwell in the simulated present of these pasts. Even when the character of a feature film's story as past is expressly and repeatedly emphasized, the tense of its representation remains the present.

The film *Goodfellas* by Martin Scorsese (USA, 1990) tells the story, based on actual events, of the rise and fall of a member of the Italian American Mafia in New York. Two minutes in, before the opening credits have finished, we hear the voice of Henry Hill (Ray Liotta) from off screen, reminiscing about his glory days in the Mafia. The voice-over anticipates the course of events from this retrospective perspective time and again, also later in the film, without giving away details of the story line in advance. This serves to create a distancing vis-à-vis the perspectives of all involved parties that remains in force even as the stations of an ultimately failed Mafia career are being presented from the inside. After a quarter hour that recapitulates the young Henry Hill's initiation into the Mafia's inner circle, a tracking shot through an Italian restaurant leads into the present of the recounted story. The voice from off screen introduces the personnel of the conspiratorial fellowship as music and fragments of dialogue are heard from the image space. As the camera pans the table in the middle of a restaurant where Hill and his pals are sitting, Hill describes, in retrospect, his attitude to life in those days. Of the normal people, those content with a modest livelihood, he says: "They were suckers. They had no balls." (Regarding his Mafia affiliation, he says, at the start of the film, "To me, it meant being somebody in a neighborhood full of nobodies"; at the end, having entered a witness protection program, Hill will concede, "I'm an average nobody.") A close-up of Hill is seen as the commentary is heard from off screen. The story now descends entirely into the somber ambience of the restaurant, the palette dominated by reds and blacks. Hill gets up from the table to meet an informant at the bar, where they are joined by Jimmy Conway (Robert De Niro); they are there to plan a coup. This conspiratorial exchange takes place in an acoustically and visually demarcated interior space within the larger space established in previous shots. With one cut, the scene returns to the table of the mafiosi—which functions like a stage in the middle of the restaurant—where Tommy De-Vito (Joe Pesci) holds forth. The communication at the table escalates, first menacingly, then comically, before the owner of the restaurant falls victim to a choleric outburst by DeVito.

In this sequence, as in many later ones, the film dwells entirely in the present of the situations it creates. It lingers in that present, which, at the beginning, the off-screen voice made clear is past. This perspectival tension permeates the narrative attitude of the entire film. Yet by means of its direction, it transposes the narrated events time and time again into a present past. This process is not undercut by the voice-over commentary, but on the contrary, is heightened by it. The commentary underscores the intensity of the stations in the protagonist's life outside the law—the permanent state of exception within which the film's story moves. The grammatical past tense reinforces the aesthetic present tense. A past present is not narrated from the perspective of an anticipated future; an impending future is narrated from the perspective of a present that still persists.

FILM AS EXPLORATION

In Baghdad

During the opening credits of *Heavy Metal in Baghdad* (Suroosh Alvi and Eddy Moretti, USA, Canada, 2007), a camera pans nervously back and forth, with an underlay of driving percussion, watching two men as they are issued bulletproof vests. The insert "August 2006" is faded in. Shortly after, we see a man's face in close-up. He looks directly into the camera and says: "We're in Baghdad and we're here to interview the only Iraqi heavy metal band, called Acrassicauda. We've been following them for three years. And we needed to check it out to see if they're still alive. This is risky, it's dangerous, people would say it's really fucking stupid for us to be doing this—but, you know, heavy metal rules." This shot of the film's two directors is twice interrupted by silent images from one of the band's concerts. Following the last sentence, the screen goes black for one second. Simultaneously, aggressive music starts up, introducing a seven-second clip of the same Acrassicauda performance. Band members are then introduced in words, images, and inserted text. This passage ends after a minute with a short dialogue. "How did you guys decide to start a band—a metal band?" asks a voice from off screen. One of the musicians answers: "If you really wanna know what is the attraction, look around: we are living in a heavy metal world." This is followed by a montage of shots of Baghdad by night and the band's concert shown previously. Explosions can be seen over the city; their sound mixes with the music. Again we see images from the concert, first in muted tones, then just black and white. The music stops. The screen goes black. After a full three minutes, the opening credits come to an end.

All the essential components of the film are already in play here. Conversations with the band members and fragmentary views of scenes in Baghdad (and Damascus, where the band later finds temporary exile), together with the directors' journalistic commentary, form the portrait of a group of musicians after the fall of Saddam Hussein's regime. With its concentration on the eccentric lifestyle of the band members, the film attains significance as an exemplar. The individual fate of the musicians appears as a symptom of a society that is not so much liberated as collapsing.

A half hour into *Heavy Metal in Baghdad* we see the directors sitting and smoking on a hotel balcony during the nightly curfew. Explosions are seen and heard again; a helicopter flies close to the hotel façade. A little later, accompanied by music and off-screen commentary, there follows a montage of drives through Baghdad, past shuttered shops, destroyed buildings, checkpoints, and military vehicles. At the end of this sequence, the vehicle in which the crew is riding makes an otherwise unmotivated U-turn in front of a symbol erected over the street that marks the exit from the city and drives back toward the city center—an incidental metaphor for the desperate impasse at which Iraq and its capital find themselves.

Urban Landscapes

We have encountered drives through urban spaces in some of our previous film examples as well—through Moscow in *The Bourne Supremacy*, through Los Angeles in *Zabriskie Point*, and through Mexico City in *Perpetuum Mobile*. But the *gestus* of these episodes is quite different. They have their aesthetic function within a fictional film narrative. The sequence in *Heavy Metal in Baghdad,* on the other hand, is not merely—as asserted in the film—composed of snapshots of Baghdad in the year 2006; it serves, as well, to make the real conditions inside this city visible. Even if its composition comes across as much less artificial than the comparable passages in the feature films mentioned above, it is just as much a product of the staging of sound and image. The significance of this staging, however, lies in a bringing into presence of living conditions endured by *persons* portrayed in the film, and their contemporaries, rather than *characters* in an invented story. The stories narrated here reconstruct a significant state of affairs in real history. That distinguishes a documentary film like *Heavy Metal in Baghdad* or *Mülheim (Ruhr)* from narrative feature films that can take considerable liberties with the factual—or even the possible—course of history.

Nevertheless, the focus of both overarching genres of cinema lies in a reconstruction or imagination of the reality of human action and human fate, even in cases where nonhuman agents or fabulous creatures are counted among the protagonists. The polarity in the arts between documentary representations, on one side, and fictional ones, on the other, must not cause us to overlook what nonetheless unites their different variants. In both cases these representations take an exploratory stance toward the worlds into which they grant us insight. Above all, the contrast between these methods must not cause us to overlook the degree to which films that diverge in their basic attitude toward the real can link up with and merge into one another. Cinema maintains an affair with the real, even where it presents its stories in an irrealis form.

Realities

This book is concerned primarily with the composition of feature films. A theory of film devoted primarily to the feature film must not focus exclusively on that cinematic genre, however. Just as the art of cinema cannot be grasped independently of its stance vis-à-vis the many other arts, the art of the feature film cannot be understood in isolation from the many other genres of film. This interconnection of filmic genres is the topic of the current chapter. The formal relations of the filmic process, as we have examined them up to now, have illuminated the basic potential of cinematic films: those creative possibilities that are unfolded, expanded, or neglected in one way or another in any given film. All genres of the cinema operate within this realm of possibilities. In the process, the difference between fictional and factual forms of representation takes on particular significance. One cannot understand the aesthetic potential of feature films—even and precisely feature films—if one fails to appreciate their documentary potential. Certainly the latter may remain unutilized, as happens often enough, but even where this aspect is rejected, the organization of a film relates to this dimension of the medium that remains inoperative in its particular case.

Moreover, the comparison between *Heavy Metal in Baghdad* and some of our feature films has already made plain that the polarity of documentary and fictional forms of the arts is established on the basis of a shared exploratory attitude. One set probes excerpts of *a* world; the other probes *their* world, which may stand in various relations to the world of *a* natural, social, and historical reality. Then again, this polarity should not be seen as characteristic of film alone. The visual arts, theater, and literature as well can move within this polarity in different ways. In that sense, they all belong to the exploratory arts, which include more than just the aesthetic arts. The sciences, too, proceed in an exploratory manner, after all, even if their investigations—depending on the orientation and methodology of *their* genres—are subject to entirely different requirements regarding explication and authentication. The broad spectrum of all of these (rather more) explaining or understanding, narrative or nonnarrative, reconstructing, experimenting, or imagining "arts," along with the practices with which this spectrum is linked, has its basis once again in the nature of human beings as agents that was discussed in the previous chapter. In the midst of a world that is accessible and inaccessible to them in equal measure, human beings are forced not only to keep pace with the abundance of the real—as challenging as it is overtaxing, as uplifting as it is devastating—but also to participate in its creation through their interventions.

Film has its own ways of investigating the actual and potential constellations of the real that make up the reality of human agency. The fictional feature film in particular, in its configurations, always inhabits constellations of this kind. Yet the situations through which it leads us are often anchored in particular historical epochs and take place in real-world settings. "Texas 1868": the story of *The Searchers* starts with this statement of place and time. One of the film's key settings is Monument Valley in Utah. *North by Northwest* begins in the present-day New York of its time and makes stops at UN Headquarters, Chicago's LaSalle Street Station, and finally Mount Rushmore—all locations that are easily recognizable for many viewers. *Goodfellas* opens in Brooklyn in 1955, traverses various locations in and around New York, and ends, as the closing credits note, in 1987. However, regardless of whether or to what degree fictional film narratives are inspired by true events, and whether or to what degree they play out in real or more or less meticulously reconstructed settings, all move within the incalculable space of *their* landscape in which they initiate *their* play with spaces and times. Even where they map out a complex interpretation of historical, social, or political conditions, they fashion their own cosmos.

Therein lies the difference, touched upon above, from the habitus of documentary films. Documentations make present the conditions and processes of *actual* realities in which agency is enacted. Fictions, on the other hand, make present *potential* realities in which agency is enacted, which may draw more or less near to or keep more or less of a distance from real ones. Only an exposition of this difference can explain why, in cinema—as in the other pictorial arts and in literature—the dimensions of documentation and fiction can connect in manifold ways.

Techniques of Documentation

In the description and evaluation of films, these distinctions are familiar to everyone; but the difference is not simple to pinpoint. With regard to a film like *Mülheim (Ruhr)*, if one envisions, along with the broad range of historical, ethnographic, social, and political documentation, the possibilities of a poetic documentation as well, proposing a watertight definition—or even a robust criterion for distinguishing between documentary and fictional formats—can seem a futile exercise. And, in fact, it *is* futile, as Angela Keppler writes: "Indeed, there is not a major distinction between documentary and fictional film staging, just as there is not a major distinction between 'realistic' and 'fantastical' language within feature films."[1] Instead, Keppler proposes an open series of indicators that can serve—not individually, but in various combinations—to classify a film as (more) documentary or (more) fictional. This allows us to avoid a theoretical defeatism that would otherwise amount to an absurd denial of the distinction between fictional and factual forms of representation: "The fact that we cannot indicate an overarching criterion for the existence of this distinction by no means . . . signifies that there is no such distinction. It exists because it is produced, again and again, in films and is perceived by viewers of films. It exists in the form of a particular *bundle* of indicators that take their value largely from the absence of the respective *counter-indicators*."[2]

These positive and negative combinations of indicators of various types constitute the *gestus* with which a film presents itself as (more) documentary or (more) fictional. This involves processes of staging of the respective filmic sequences that, taken together, often—though by no means always—give rise to an unequivocal distinction between documentation and fiction.

Recalling the beginning of the previous chapter, I would like to call attention again to the fact that neither filmic documentations nor feature films necessarily proceed narratively. Not every nonnarrative film proceeds in a documentary fashion. And not every documentary film proceeds in a narrative fashion. Most do, however. They are structured in a narrative manner, they are accompanied by narrative passages or recount the stories of persons affected; in *Heavy Metal in Baghdad*, each of these levels has a crucial function. Demonstrating the factuality of the conditions and events presented and reproduced plays a decisive role here. What is shown and said cannot derive solely from the director's imagination. Documentary films assert the claim of reproducing aspects of the reality that existed or exists outside of the film—aspects that were or are significant (directly or indirectly) for the human beings involved, their deeds, and the consequences that befall them. Whether a film merely *presents itself* in documentary fashion or *is*, in fact, documentary is determined not least by its reference to the real locations, times, and persons on which it reports. It is with these factors, above all, that the series of images visible on the screen must *originate* in the case of true documentation. If *Heavy Metal in Baghdad* had been filmed in, say, Beirut, rather than Baghdad and Damascus (the actual stations in the lives of the actual members of Acrassicauda), it might have met the standards of a biopic devoted to this exotic band, but not those of a documentation of the situation in Iraq in 2003.

Even documentary films can only offer excerpted details of the realities to which they refer. In that sense, they too present a filmically constructed image and thus a specific interpretation of the respective reality being represented. This excerpt quality, however, is precisely the point of the process. What is meant to be presented, after all, are conditions and events that existed or exist independently of their being brought into presence filmically. Documentary films inevitably select what they present from the standpoint of what is relevant for the respective subject matter, as well as what will be comprehensible for the audience. In so doing, they map out a specific perspective on the conditions, events, and actors presented in them, offering a view of the respective circumstances that may be enlightening or distorting, polemical or reserved. This opens up the perspectival differences discussed in the previous chapter, differences that are characteristic of historical, artistic, and other reporting forms of representation.

Films also assert a documentary claim by means of a diverse set of authentication strategies. These are meant to make credible that what is shown in the filmic arrangement really happened, in all relevant respects, as shown. They are meant to make clear that the state of affairs being presented could be (or could have been) witnessed by any observer. Among these strategies are a filmic insistence on the contingency of what is seen and heard; the precise indication of the place and time of the events that are presented; their classification in terms of geographical, historical, and social contexts; the presentation of witnesses; the emphasis on the documentarian's status as an eyewitness; and the presentation of external sources that are meant to substantiate the events and the film's interpretation of them. Documentary films' particular exploratory claim is evident here. Their *gestus* consists in presenting an *informative* perspective on extrafilmic circumstances, which are depicted as they *actually* stand. The associated truth claim lies in the assertion made through the form of these films (not least by means of their respective authentication strategies), that the situations presented (in the aspects in which they are shown) were or are *exactly* as they appear in the film.

Whether a film *asserts* a documentary claim is recognizable from the film's formal attributes. Whether a film *fulfills* the documentary *gestus* that it asserts and *to what extent* it fulfills it, on the other hand, cannot be ascertained from its formal attributes alone. This ultimately demands the judgment of the audience, which must draw on its own knowledge of the world and thus invariably on additional mediating testimonies and sources. As with other forms of reportage, judgment about the documentary quality of a film depends on comparative assessments.

Documentary films, in summary, are those that present situations and events as ones that took place independently of the film production at exactly the same locations, at exactly the same times, and with the participation of exactly the same persons as are visible in the film sequences. These events are presented as ones that occurred in a sequence and in a context that were not subject to the direction of a screenplay and its realization. Films that match this description bring into presence domains of the reality in which human agency is enacted (or domains of the real that are meaningful for human experience, cognition, and action in other respects) in dimensions of their facticity that are predefined for the filmic process.

A Double Promise

The prerogative of documentary films lies in a *gestus* formulated by means of their specific dramaturgy. It is in the way a film of this type presents itself to its viewers that it lays claim to being proof of an external reality that is largely independent of the filmic arrangement. As in the case of photography, this claim may be realized or—whether the intent be manipulative or artistic—it may remain unrealized. Like photography (inasmuch as the latter adheres to its realistic *gestus* examined in chapter 3), documentary films make present a past state of affairs of the extrafilmic world. Like most photographs, they refer to the way something was. In its documentary methods, film plays out its own photographic nature in a particular way.

But, indeed, it *plays* it out in a particular way. The temporal difference, analyzed in the previous chapter, between filmic and other forms of reconstruction and narration remains in force even here—indeed, especially here. Whatever they present, documentary films, too, convey it in a temporal mode that translates *what was* into the present tense of their presentation. Whether *Mülheim (Ruhr)* or *Heavy Metal in Baghdad*—documentary films of this and other types transpose former times and/or continuous presents into the present of their audiovisual movement; the stronger the artistic orientation of the production, the more this operation applies. Yet the mere fact that they are composed of filmic recordings is by no means the source of their documentary *gestus*. The fact that something somewhere was in front of the camera does not, by a long stretch, make a film a documentary. The character of a film emerges, rather, from specific techniques of sound and image composition—techniques by which the documentary film distinguishes itself from other film genres.

The *gestus* of documentary cinema can be reduced to a common denominator. To use the language of our analysis of the relations between film and photography in the *Blow-Up* discussion in chapter 3: documentary cinema makes its audience a double promise—the one that is inherent in the form of photography and, simultaneously, the one that is inherent in the form of film. Film itself, however, makes no such double promise, if only because feature films, while they always claim to keep the second promise, frequently forgo any claim to fulfill the first. They make only the modest promise to exploit unreservedly the imaginative potential of cinema, without committing to represent conditions of extrafilmic reality.

Techniques of Fiction

Just as there are feature films that manage without narrative modalities, there also those that do not make use of the techniques of fiction. To forgo both does not necessarily lend a film a documentary character, however. A film like *Five* is not a documentary because, beyond the evidence of its sonic and visual appearing, the location and time of its creation are not crucial factors. *Hamburger Lektionen*, but also the short film by Iñárritu interpreted in chapter 4, are examples of films that despite their documentary elements exhibit something closer to the format of feature films. Moreover, fictions of a nonnarrative or not exclusively narrative sort (e.g., models, mythical creatures, thought experiments) are employed in the arts as well as the sciences. Nevertheless, fictional narration is the general rule for the constitution of feature films—though one that has some notable exceptions.

Fictional narratives have one thing in common across the various art forms. They project worlds that do not exist and never existed *like this* (and, in some cases, that could not exist or could never have existed)— worlds that are only accessible via perception of the art object. Feature films bring the formal constitution of their medium to fruition in a particular way in this regard. Their key aspects, writes James Conant,

> are (what Heidegger might have called) the *worldhood of the world of a movie* and *the mode of disclosure of such a world*. I will say: for something to be a movie it must offer us *glimpses of a world*. That is, in order for something to be a movie, first, it must visually *present a world* into which it can invite us and in which we can become absorbed; and, second, our mode of absorption must be one of *watching* it: we *see* what happens in that world.[3]

Conant draws a distinction between the aesthetics of the feature film, conceived in this way, and other instances of filmic imagery:

> According to the terminology I will employ here, the world of a home movie is not a movie-world. The world depicted in a home movie is our world— that is, the world that we who watch the home movie inhabit—it is a representation of that world as photographed by a camera. The being of the world of the home movie is in this respect ontologically akin to that of the newsreel and the documentary. The presentation of the world of (what I am calling) a movie presupposes a nexus of unity different in kind from that which unifies the sequences of images in any of the aforementioned genres of non-fiction film.[4]

It should be noted, however, that a documentary film produced for the cinema can likewise put the "worldhood of the world" on view. In its way, it can produce a higher rhythm through which it allows fragmentary glimpses into an extrafilmic world; in so doing, it too can give rise to specific audiovisual attractions, such as by all means occurs in *Heavy Metal in Baghdad* or *Mülheim (Ruhr)*. Yet in the nature of their "nexus of unity," that is, the overall temporal and spatial organization of their visual and acoustic progression, feature films are distinct not only from the many other instances of filmic imagery, but in particular from the techniques of an unequivocally documentary cinema. Their worlds arise from the inventions of their form.

Fictional film stories are characterized by the fact that, at the very least, they leave open the question of whether the course of actions and events they depict ever took place outside of the presented narrative. Many of them leave no doubt that this is anything but the case. Like documentation, fiction is first of all a *gestus* in which the events on the screen are offered up—and which the audience can accept or reject.

Much can be fictionalized in feature films: locations and their spatial relations, temporal and causal relations, characters and situations depicted, and above all plots and story lines. The linkage of some or all of these factors occurs within the framework of the particular possibilities offered by filmic narration. In their fictional form, these possibilities enable a certain kind of play, not only with the particular events and conflicts that are represented, but with the perspectives on them that are opened up. This play is the crucial motor of the artistic generation of worlds in the cinema. Fictional films lead us into an audiovisual space that does not (primarily) present extracts from the real world of action, but rather (primarily) opens up opportunities to explore a world sui generis. In composing a fictional story, it is not enough merely to contrive a more or less unreal situation; one must devise an inner-fictional *interconnection* of scenes that are embedded in the horizon of an imagined world (and, often, one that is imaginary to a greater or lesser degree).

Fictional films, in summary, are those that present a series of occurrences, connected for the most part via narrative linkages, that never happened *just this way* (with exactly *these* twists and turns) or that could never have happened except on the screen. Any temporal and spatial localization of the narrative and what it recounts in the historical world may be left more or less open or may remain altogether absent. In this way, narrative feature films place on view potential realities of human deeds and consequences, experiences and travails. They enable a variable process of coming to self-awareness on the part of the audience about biographical and historical, individual and collective, probable and improbable, situations, often with exemplary significance.

Questions of Style

Of course, theory must not be more rigid than filmic practice itself in handling the distinctions highlighted here. Any sort of purism would be misplaced. Films are "fictional" or "documentary" if they *predominantly* operate in one or the other mode. *Elements* of one approach can occur in the other without this necessarily constituting a borderline case. The presence or absence of actors, of figures that look directly into the camera, of film music, jump cuts, sophisticated lighting and color control, an elaborately composed higher rhythm, or continuous off-screen narration—none of these or any other factor alone is grounds for assigning a film to one or the other genre. My discussion of a specific *"gestus"* and a specific "staging" characteristic of documentary films points out, following Keppler, that the distinction between fictional and factual films is not least a stylistic one. Films indicate by their style—or more precisely, by their bundle of stylistic attributes—whether they want to be understood as (primarily) fictional inquiries into a reality that they have created or as documentary presentations of a reality that they have sought out.[5]

Documentary films can also take inventive approaches, and fictional films can follow documentary ones. A feature film like Michelangelo Antonioni's *L'Eclisse* takes a documentary attitude, at the end of the film, toward the locations where the story that was told up to that point had unfolded. *JFK* (Oliver Stone, USA, 1991) and *Thirteen Days* (Roger Donaldson, USA, 2000) are feature films that hew closely to times and locations of historical events. *Zelig* (Woody Allen, USA, 1983) and *Forrest Gump* (Robert Zemeckis, USA, 1994) incorporate documentary material (estranged to varying degrees from its historical context) into their fictional story. *Fahrenheit 9/11* (Michael Moore, USA, 2004) combines documentary material and speculative commentary in a polemical essay film that, with its use of background music and inner dialogues ascribed to the American president, also contains inventive passages. *Le Gai Savoir* (Jean-Luc Godard, France, 1969) presents a chaotic montage of contemporary images, texts, and voices from the media, shot through with political and philosophical, poetic and metapoetic, dialogues that combines filmic self-exploration with an associative diagnosis of the present moment in history.

Even films with an unequivocal claim to documentary status can take inventive approaches to a considerable degree. The film *The Green Wave* by Ali Samadi Ahadi (Germany, 2011) deals with the short and brutal period of social and political upheaval in Iran before and after the presidential election in the early summer of 2009. The film's documentary *gestus* is marked by a multilayered composition. In a calculated interplay, it makes use of images from the Iranian media, plays back interviews with participants, most living in exile by the time the film is made, and returns again and again (with increasing frequency as events escalate) to a montage of Handycam shots of demonstrators and passersby. In addition, animated scenes tell the story of a young man and a young woman who are caught up in the upheaval in Iran. (There is a formal relationship here with an almost fully animated documentary like Ari Folman's *Waltz with Bashir* [Israel, France, Germany, 2008]). All of the internal monologues voiced in the animated scenes are compiled from blogs published during the demonstrations by participants. Even in its fictional elements, *The Green Wave* presents a reconstruction that is aligned with factual events; its primary concern is less the events before and after the manipulated election than the activists' reactions to the repression to which they were subjected from various sides.

Loss of Control

There are feature films, furthermore, that not only have an unmistakable basis in fact, but that present themselves in a documentary vein. *United 93* (Paul Greengrass, USA, 2006) dramatizes the events surrounding the crash of the passenger flight hijacked by terrorists on September 11, 2001. The aircraft was en route to Washington, D.C., where it was evidently to have been crashed into the Capitol, when it went down over Pennsylvania. Thus the film deals with an extremely well-known event, extensively documented in the media after 9/11, an event whose outcome is familiar to almost everyone, even if the events inside the aircraft can only be partially reconstructed. Like the firefighters who risked or lost their lives in the ruins of the Twin Towers (to whom Oliver Stone dedicated a justificatory melodrama, *World Trade Center* [USA, 2006]), the passengers on this flight are part of the process of American legend formation, not only because they left behind poignant messages for their loved ones, but above all because during the flight, in full knowledge that they were the victims of deadly commandos, they forcibly defended themselves. The plot of the film is an air disaster that, for political reasons, became an American myth.

United 93 satisfies neither a longing for a reassuring heroization nor the expectations of an action-packed disaster film. There are no stars among the cast, and several of the actors are nonprofessionals, some of whom were personally involved in the events of 9/11. The dialogue is partly improvised. There are no heroes. Only a few of the characters are referred to by name. The film takes a neutral stance even vis-à-vis the figures of the terrorists. Film music is heard only at the beginning and the end. The film entirely forgoes spectacular imagery; even the iconic images from 9/11 are only quoted from a great distance. A restless handheld camera traverses the mostly chaotic scenes (chaotic also from an acoustic standpoint). In a mode of reporting by showing, *United 93* captures how it was or how it may have been. By refusing to draw any political conclusions, the film communicates an attitude of respect toward everyone (even the perpetrators) caught up in the dynamic of terror.

Certainly the key dramaturgical operation here lies in the filmic treatment of space and time. Paul Greengrass and his team created an introverted disaster film. What would be the prelude in the typical films of the genre constitutes the main event in this case. The interior of the aircraft is not privileged as the primary setting of the action in *United 93*. Indeed, the spaces in which the film lingers the longest are the regional and national air traffic control centers, five of them in all, as well as the Newark airport tower. The prehistory of the hijacking takes up the greatest share of the plot. Thus, the narrated time of the film conforms, at times, exactly to the real time of the events of that day. The plot is at first entirely dominated by the routine of aviation into which initial irritations and fissures begin to creep, little by little, about which the passengers in the aircraft know nothing at first. In the control rooms, often darkened, with their countless monitors, the film pursues an audiovisual ethnography of institutional communication under increasingly irregular conditions. In an unreal environment that is literally shielded from immediate danger, real horror spreads at an almost casually unhurried pace. The unreality of a reality monitored by technical instruments makes the incursion of the historical event seem that much more real. From the margins, the film dramatizes not so much terror itself as the disbelief, the denial of the truth, and, finally, its acknowledgment that terror brings in its wake.

While in *United 93* it is above all the protagonists who suffer a loss of control, in Abbas Kiarostami's *Nema-ye Nazdik* (*Close-Up*; Iran, France, 1990), it is chiefly the viewers who are subjected to a persistent irritation. This film, too, is based on real events. It deals, in the main, with the trial of an unemployed cineast who deceives a Tehran family into believing that he is the director Mohsen Makhmalbaf and wants to make a film inside their home. The narrative is carried by cast members who participated in the actual incident and are playing themselves. In this way, the film moves along a borderline between documentation and fiction. What develops is an ambiguous comedy of mistaken identity whose impact is tragicomic. In an improvisational form, it addresses the ways in which art and life mirror each other, as well as the power of cinema itself to open up worlds.

References to the World

The fact that the various operations of documentary and fictional cinema can intersect, link up, and combine in such multifarious ways is indicative, yet again, of the exploratory character that the cinematic genres share. Their distinct references to the world have a common root in the exploration of real or invented realities that concern—or could concern—the audience, in some way, in its lived reality. Herein lies the primary aesthetic promise of the cinema, which our interpretation of the image analysis in *Blow-Up* has already underscored: "Whatever a film promises, rightly or wrongly, it keeps the promise to be a variation on the human being-in-the-world—and thus a variety of the same."[6] Whether or to whatever degree a cinematic film also encompasses photography's promise—or toys with it—it brings into presence, in its inner organization, aspects of the worldliness of the world. The directions taken by this exploration can vary enormously. It may focus predominantly on the real world, on the universe of an invented world, even on the filmic process itself—or all of these at once. *Close-Up* operates at all of these levels in almost every moment. But however a film might isolate these dimensions one from the other or place them in relation to each other, it always gives rise to the horizon of a world within its own horizon. Thus Dudley Andrew writes, with reference to André Bazin: "Real cinema has a relation to the real."[7]

This formulation must be properly understood, however. For the cinema's affair with "the real" has nothing to do with a disposition to aesthetic realism. Even documentary films can bring the surreal quality of real-world conditions into sharp relief. In *Heavy Metal in Baghdad*, the members of Acrassicauda refer to a "Song for Saddam" that they had to perform to circumvent the censors under the old regime. The song's refrain rhymes "Hussein" with "insane." Feature films, all the more, can be subject, in their narrative style, to direction that is (more) "realistic" or "surrealistic," "fantastic" or "documentary," "grotesque" or "veristic," and so forth. In the cinema, there is room for films like *L'Age d'Or* (Luis Buñuel, France, 1930), *A Night at the Opera, Bringing Up Baby, Hellzapoppin'* (Henry C. Potter, USA, 1941), *Star Wars* (George Lucas, USA, 1977), or *Brazil* (Terry Gilliam, UK, 1985), as well as for *M* (Fritz Lang, Germany, 1931), *The Grapes of Wrath* (John Ford, USA, 1940), *Ossessione* (Luchino Visconti, Italy, 1943), *The Wrong Man* (Alfred Hitchcock, USA, 1956), *Benny's Video* (Michael Haneke, Austria, Switzerland, 1992), and *Elephant* (Gus Van Sant, USA, 2003). Traces and reflections of realities known to humankind from history and the present can be found everywhere, even when feature films probe deep into unknown worlds. In *Alien* (Ridley Scott, USA, 1979) and its four sequels, this is palpable throughout. A 3D spectacular like *Avatar* conceives an ecotopia, at once primitive and futuristic, whose inhabitants are equipped with a body part that they can use like a data cable to log in to a spiritual network. An all-ages entertainment film like *Ice Age* deals with nothing less than the collective survival of climate catastrophe. In their attractionism, animated films of the old and new type follow a principle of carnivalization in which the causal, temporal, and narrative orders otherwise in effect are capriciously turned on their heads—and precisely thereby made present in subtle, subversive, and sometimes also reflexive ways.

In light of these circumstances, it proves highly misleading to view the artistic potential of the feature film as bound to a doctrine of realism, as has frequently been the case in the history of film theory. In its basic formal disposition, cinema is indifferent with regard to an opposition—however it might be understood—between aesthetic realism and antirealism.[8] As in the other arts, the spectrum of its creative possibilities remains open and indeterminate—and the same holds true for the scope of its exploratory possibilities.

These structures of the cinema remain operative, even in light of the transition from analogue to digital image production. Particularly for the feature film, the basal forms of audiovisual appearing have not changed radically as a result of this shift.[9] New possibilities of aesthetic composition have been added without the old ones losing their power. The technological evolution of the digital image has not resulted in a break with the traditional situation of the *perception* of films in the cinema, even if some of the *films* engendered in this context do indeed mark a caesura in the history of cinema—as many films before them have done as well. The digital evolution has not brought about an aesthetic revolution. Compared to the transition to the sound film and, later, to color, it has been almost innocuous. Films like *Ice Age*, *Avatar*, or *Sin City* (Robert Rodriguez and Frank Miller, USA, 2005) are feature films in the same sense as *The Searchers* or *North by Northwest*, even if their production style is completely different.

The End

At the beginning of Francis Ford Coppola's *Apocalypse Now*, the screen is black. After five seconds, we hear a synthetically produced sound that is reminiscent of the sound of helicopter blades. After twelve seconds, the screen lightens. We see a thick palm forest. The sound persists. Smoke billows from the lower right edge of the image. After twenty-three seconds—the sound gets louder—a helicopter flies past from left to right, directly in front of the camera. Yellowish clouds of smoke partially obscure the view of the jungle. We continue to hear the slapping of the rotor blades. At the same time, the song "The End" by the Doors begins. As the song's opening notes are heard, the landing skids of a second helicopter cut across the image. After forty seconds the forest is engulfed in a wall of fire, and the words of the song begin: "This is the end / Beautiful friend / This is the end / My only friend, the end" and so on. The scene dissolves in dark smoke. The silhouettes of two helicopters move across the image in both directions. The face of Captain Willard (Martin Sheen), shot from above, is faded into this diffuse background. With eyes wide open, he stares lazily into the void. Our view of his face is overlaid with the rapid spinning movement of a fan. With that, the mix of image and sound is established that will dominate the remaining two and a half minutes of the film's opening sequence. The burning jungle, the helicopters intersecting the image, the increasingly realistic sound of their rotors, the spinning of the fan on the ceiling of the hotel room where Willard lies in agony, the music and lyrics of the song—all of this is fused into a nightmarish sequence. It becomes nearly impossible to distinguish between what is happening on screen and off, in the character's situation and in his imagination. Finally, the camera travels through the captain's room up to the blinds hanging in front of the window and gazes between the slats at a street scene. Willard's voice is heard from off screen. "Saigon" is the first word we hear.

The film begins at an existential end point for its main character. But it will be 148 minutes, in the original version, and 194 minutes in the director's cut (*Apocalypse Now Redux, USA, 2001*), before the film reaches its end. Already from the beginning, it intones the conflation of projection and reality that dominates the outlook of nearly all the characters in the face of the war's brutality. The impenetrability of the filmic space lays bare the uncontrollability of the military events. This film, too, returns at the end to the composition of its opening sequence. The killing sequence described in chapter 4 is accompanied by an isolated passage from the song by the Doors, at the end of which the sound of the rotor blades heard at the start of the film is quoted for a moment. When it is over, as he leaves the murderous colony of Colonel Kurtz, Willard stares with an absent gaze into the darkness. Once more the voice of the slain colonel murmurs the words "the horror, the horror." As this is happening, the silhouettes of two helicopters move—with no motivation at the level of the plot—across the image in the opposite direction. The preverberation of the introductory dream sequence becomes a reverberation of the film's central formal elements. Even when cinema hallucinates, it contends with the madness and the reality of the human world.

FILM AS IMAGINATION

At Bakersfield

In the middle of Hitchcock's *North by Northwest*, Roger Thornhill (Cary Grant) and Eve Kendall (Eva Marie Saint) arrive at the station in Chicago after their rendezvous in a night train from New York. With Kendall's help, Thornhill succeeds in remaining unnoticed by the police who have a warrant for his arrest as an alleged murderer. Thornhill wants to meet George Kaplan, the man for whom his pursuers have mistaken him. Eve Kendall, the beautiful double agent who knows that this man Kaplan doesn't really exist, offers to arrange a meeting with the unseen third party. After consulting with her associates, she tells Thornhill to take the Greyhound bus to Indianapolis and get out after an hour and a half at a certain stop; George Kaplan will be waiting. After their passionate time together, they say a chilly goodbye—much to Thornhill's chagrin. Conscious of having led him into a trap, Kendall gazes fearfully after Thornhill, who exits to the left of the screen.

Next begins the cornfield scene described in the first chapter, which was filmed near Bakersfield, California. Of course, to reach the actual shooting location by bus, Thornhill would have had to travel for days. But this does not matter in a feature film. Its fiction is not bound to the real continuity of space and time. It can compose the landscape of its world by interleaving any locations it desires. And so Thornhill stands in the middle of an open and, at first, largely uneventful setting. He waits, looks around him, swallows the dust that billows up from passing vehicles. He takes a taciturn farmer, who only wants to catch the next bus, for the ominous George Kaplan, ignorant as yet of the threat posed to him by the aircraft that can already be heard in the distance. At first slowly, almost as if in slow motion, the dramatic action, anticipated by the audience but not by the protagonist, gains momentum until, finally, Thornhill succeeds once more in escaping grave peril. In this episode, too, a rather mad game with the topoi of suspense cinema develops. Throughout the film, this game is linked to an exhibition of the director's various obsessions and to countless cinematic sleights of hand.

An Illusionistic Interpretation

In the many extant interpretations of this film, this self-referential quality of its staging has frequently been noted.[1] George Wilson's discussion of the film provides a case in point: "*North by Northwest* presents us with a kind of wry apologia for the sort of illusionistic art—more specifically, for the sort of illusionistic cinema—that Hitchcock, paradigmatically, has always practiced."[2] Clearly, this interpretation contradicts itself. An oblique *apologia* for cinematic illusionism cannot be reconcilable with the *illusionism* that is ostensibly demonstrated in a film like *North by Northwest*. After all, an exhibition of its own filmic *techniques* would undermine the illusionistic *effects* that, according to Wilson's interpretation, those techniques engender. If, on the other hand, one assumes that normal observers give themselves up to an aesthetic illusion while professional interpreters are uniquely equipped to recognize the underlying artistic calculations, it would follow that the film spectacularly fails to achieve what Wilson attributes to it. Hitchcock would have failed, in that case, to "present" his own sleights of hand to the audience—a presentation that Wilson is wholly correct in saying constitutes a major part of this film's attraction.

Deleting the word "illusionistic" from the sentence quoted above dispels the contradiction in Wilson's interpretation. The contradiction arises because Wilson advocates a film-theoretical illusionism that necessarily misapprehends the character of this feature film, and not only this one. For Wilson, this position is tied to the idea of the "transparency" of the filmic image: "The function of transparency is to induce in the spectators the impression of seeing the given fictional world through the screen as directly as they see the actual world through their front windows."[3] Yet this outlook makes it impossible to come to terms with the subtleties of sound and image and thus with cinema's specific attractionism. It is of little help when Wilson remarks, with regard to Hitchcock: "It is a fundamental aspect of classical narration that seeks, in effect, to collapse the distinction between perception of the world and perception of the film in its own fashion."[4] How could such a collapse of the distinction between filmic and extrafilmic events be possible? How could it be possible to take a film seriously, in its proper form, if its perception depends on the belief that its choreography is directly tied in with the course of the world?

Unlike the preceding ones, this chapter has a predominantly critical aim—that of refuting film-theoretical illusionism. Building on the phenomenology of films' appearing in the cinema that has been developed up to now, I will propose an alternative interpretation. This analysis will focus exclusively on the narrative feature film. As a motto, we can preface it with a slightly modified version of George Wilson's statement cited above: *North by Northwest* presents us with a kind of wry apologia for the sort of *imaginative* art—more specifically, for the sort of *imaginative* cinema—that Hitchcock, paradigmatically, has always practiced.

The Figure of the Illusionist

Certainly, the illusionists of film theory also aspire to come to terms with the specific attraction of the filmic image. They wish to explain the immersive power of the cinema. They wish to elucidate why we, as viewers of feature films, can be absorbed in a certain way by events on the screen. Their theories are devoted to this powerful motivation. Illusion explains immersion: this is their fundamental thesis. By contrast, I wish to show that the fascination of the cinematic film can be explained without

illusionistic impulses. "Immersion without illusion" or, put more posi-
tively, "imagination rather than illusion"—these mottos point the way.

For the purposes of this critique, I introduce the fictional character of
the illusionist. My argumentation is directed not so much against individual
exponents of film-theoretical illusionism, but rather against certain basic
assumptions that they advocate in various combinations. The "illusionist"
thus assumes the role of a challenger, similar to the figure of the "skep-
tic" in the field of epistemology who—to the extent possible—is meant to
be reduced to silence. Of course, in these controversies, even assigning a
theoretical position to a (more) skeptical or (more) antiskeptical camp is
frequently contentious. The situation is no different in discussing the point
or pointlessness of illusionism in art theory in general and in film theory in
particular. From the point of view of radical anti-illusionism, which is ultimately the tendency of this book's investigations, traces of illusionism are
sometimes at work in the philosophy of art and, in particular, in film theory,
precisely where a theory believes it is resisting illusionism's overtures.[5]

This anti-illusionism is comparatively radical for a simple reason: it
contests the notion that an aesthetic illusion is a *necessary* element—and
in that sense a *constitutive* element—of an intensive experience of the feature film, no matter the type. I do not make the claim, however, that an
illusionistic experience of films is *impossible*. I do not dispute that this experience occurs in the cinema, nor do I make any assumptions about how
widespread this experience is. Yet I do contend that film's aesthetic potential fully unfolds solely on this side of the process of illusion formation.
Thus, my thesis is also directed against moderate illusionists who wish
to grant aesthetic illusion a merely supporting role, though usually an
inevitable one, in the experience of cinema. For them, too, the possibility
of this illusion is part and parcel of film's basic artistic potential. For the
moderate illusionists, it always suggests itself in the cinema, even if it can
be frequently circumvented, temporarily interrupted, and even suspended
entirely by certain forms of film.[6]

Illusion and Immersion

The illusionist's central figure of thought is the conception that films that
are capable of fascinating their audience instill the belief, at least to some

degree, that what happens on the screen is actually occurring in the moment when it appears. Viewers perceive what is represented as if it were real. In this as-if mode, they encounter a reality that is accessible only by sight, hearing, and bodily sensation, but in which they cannot actively intervene. For the illusionist, this shows the "transparency" of the filmic image: it allows viewers to be present and involved in an event that is presented in the here and now of the filmic progression, with numerous trappings of authenticity. This, the illusionist asserts, is why the filmic moving image takes us along in such an exceptional way. It is aesthetic illusion that enables immersion, which is heightened in comparison to the other arts.

This aesthetic semblance, in the illusionist's understanding, is anything but a deception. The audiovisual appearing of a film, to this way of thinking, by no means leads the audience astray. The audience knows, after all, that what it is watching is "only a movie"; but it watches in such a way that it gives itself up to the film's performance in a particular fashion. In the process, the audience acquires many true beliefs about the state of this or that fictional world, even if, for dramaturgical reasons, it is occasionally led around by the nose. With regard to the cornfield scene in *North by Northwest*, the viewers assume correctly that Roger Thornhill wants to meet George Kaplan. This belief is true, even though, as it later turns out, it is not true that there is really a person by the name of George Kaplan in the world of this film. The impression of reality in the cinema builds on and sustains itself by means of a corresponding game with the beliefs held by the viewers. For the duration of the film, they must be prepared to believe in the reality of what, by the nature of its staging, it makes them believe.

For authors like Kendall Walton and George Wilson, this understanding of film is tied to the notion of "imagining seeing." As viewers, according to this conception, we imagine that the character embodied by Cary Grant is Roger Thornhill, who works in advertising, is twice divorced and trapped in a peculiar mother fixation, a man who is pursued by various powers as a spy and a murderer, but saves himself in the end in the arms of the third Mrs. Thornhill. In the cornfield scene, we imagine how Thornhill, standing there without a clue, swallowing dust, is attacked by the airplane and ultimately finds refuge under a tanker truck. We imagine him as a real person. This, the illusionist tells us, is how the fiction of this and every other feature film (or at least every other "classical" feature film) works. In the process of being observed, the film's *characters* attain the lives of *persons*, and we experience their actions and fates accordingly; what happens to them matters to us as if it were part of our world.[7]

Such a theory of the imagined seeing of images has a considerable shortcoming, however. It operates with a naïve concept of seeing that cannot do justice to the ontology of works of art. It is not the case— not in the cinema and not in the theater—that we see people on the screen or on the stage and must somehow additionally imagine them as embodiments of particular characters. Rather, our seeing in the cinema and in the theater incorporates, from the outset, knowledge about the representational character of the events on the screen and on the stage. Our seeing and hearing in these settings always already has the character of an understanding apprehending.[8] Because, in the cinema, we are attuned to the fact that we are following an artistic presentation, we *see* Roger Thornhill standing in the dust of the Midwest, where the actor portraying him never set foot during the shooting of the film. The fact that characters are embodied by actors and are thus visible in their representation simply belongs to the rules of the artistic game to which performance, performers, and audience are subject in equal measure. Familiarity with the ground rules of this game colors our seeing and hearing even when one or the other of the conventional rules is broken. Whoever understands this game's rules and its rule breaking perceives what occurs in its fictional worlds because these worlds are where the occurrences are presented.

The illusionist, on the other hand, commits spectators in the cinema (and the audiences addressed by many other arts) to a massive forgetting of representation. This misstep is also responsible for Wilson's dilemma: an immersive participation in filmic events can supposedly only set in if their formal organization is largely disregarded. After all, the illusion— seen through cognitively, but let through aesthetically—can only come about if the spectators, while they are looking at the filmic image, also look through it, as it were. The involved perception of a film, according to illusionism, cannot afford for any attention—or at least not more than a minimum—to be paid to the film's operation. To attentively *follow* a film means to renounce attentively following the *film*.

Imagination Not Illusion

These art-theoretical paradoxes are disastrous, but fortunately also un-
necessary. They are dispelled as soon as the imaginative composition of
the film itself is recognized and acknowledged. This imagination has its
origins not in an aesthetic semblance, but in an aesthetic appearing. It is
given along with the basic formal properties of a film. When spectators
follow a film, they follow its imaginative presentation. When they are
captivated by a film, it is the film's imaginative presentation that captivates them. Illusionism's forgetting of representation can and must be suspended.[9] Imagination, not illusion, explains immersion.

This thesis only recapitulates the investigations carried out up to now.
The first two chapters presented the basal operation of film as that of
opening up an "imagined space" and an "imagined time." Chapter 3 described the artistic image as a form of "articulated imagination" that is
transferred into a heightened "zone of imagination" in cinema's space
of sound and image. Building on these determinations, chapter 4 underscored the particular virtuality of a film's audiovisual movement. Chapter 5 compared the imaginative capacity of film with that of literature.
Chapter 6 emphasized the particular imaginative disposition of fictional
feature films in comparison with a documentary exploration of the world
in the cinema. The concept of filmic imagination developed in these steps
is a formal concept. Not only explicitly fantastic films like *Céline and
Julie Go Boating* (*Céline et Julie vont en bateau*; Jacques Rivette, France,
1974) or *Blade Runner* (Ridley Scott, USA, 1982) proceed imaginatively,
in this sense. Rather, this is a property of narrative feature films in general,
regardless of how much or how little their fictions might depart from the
probabilities of the historical world.

The "imagination" of a film, understood in this way, does not mean
merely what might be imagined in it. Rather, the concept stands for the relationship between representation and what is represented. It denotes the
continuity, crucial for the dynamics of the feature film, between putting-
in-the-picture and what-is-put-in-the-picture (together with its auditory
dimensions). It is by virtue of their imagination, in this sense, that films
open up room-for-play for the imagination of the spectators as well. The
latter remains dependent on the former, however. The spectators' imagination, that is, remains dependent on how situations and characters are

presented to us in the movement of a film—which is to say, how they are represented there. *We* are not the ones, when viewing *North by Northwest*, who imagine Roger Thornhill as a human being who has to endure all sorts of adventures; *the film* presents this to us in the choreography of its staging. It doesn't seem to us as if Thornhill were standing and waiting in a mostly empty rural landscape; the film *shows* him to us in this situation. We do not *imagine* that we see a character that only exists on the screen; we *see* him in action within the filmic narrative. We can save ourselves the theoretical duplication of an "imagined seeing" because film does not burden viewers with it. Film lets nothing of the sort even come up. On the strength of its imagination, film represents and puts on display whatever we find presented in its process.

The situation is no different with regard to pictorial representations in general. Images do not afford us the illusion of a real presence of the relations they present to us; they provide us with real, unsubstitutable *views* of whatever it is they show—and precisely in this way they expand the spectrum of human perception. The filmic moving image participates in these relations after its own fashion. With regard to interconnections between the auditory and visual dimensions of a film, the first three chapters have already made clear just how real the virtuality of filmic space and also of filmic time truly is. Indeed, for spectators in the cinema, it is not *as if* they were in the midst of a film's audiovisual events. They *are* in the midst of events as they follow a film by seeing, hearing, and sensing. They are there, ideally with their senses alert, as the film completes its course. There is no illusion that deters them from perceiving the intricacies of the filmic staging.

Photography and Film, Again

In order to clarify the significance of my argument against illusionism in film theory, it is worth returning yet again to the relationship between photography and film. After all, the question of whether a theoretical perspective on the arts of cinema can prove fruitful is decided on the basis of this relationship. Here we must rebut a series of errors that have one thing in common: they misconstrue the indisputable relationship between the two media. The variants of an exaggerated realism have their roots here, but so too do the temptations of illusionism. Five fallacies lead down the wrong track in this regard.

The first, the *genealogical* fallacy, appears fairly innocuous: because film emerged from the technology of photography, the two media are intimately related, also from an aesthetic standpoint. Of the classical film theorists, Siegfried Kracauer probably gave this view its most resolute articulation; we find it in a weaker form in André Bazin.[10] Yet the affair with "the real," which the feature film, too, maintains, must not be understood in the sense of a normative realism, as the previous chapter made clear. As much as photography and film have in common, from an aesthetic point of view, they are not "intimately" related.

This becomes evident in light of the second fallacy, the *technologistic* fallacy, which appears similar enough to the first as to be easily confused with it: because the filmic image, from a technological standpoint, consists of a succession of photographic images, it shares the realistic *gestus* of photographic images. Even leaving aside for a moment the fact that not every feature film today consists of photographic images, this thesis arises from an inadmissible crossover from the technology of the filmic image to its aesthetics. Even a conventional film whose image world is *generated* by "photography plus movement" and thus, from a technical standpoint, *consists* of a sequence of photographic images is by no means bound, on these grounds, to the *gestus* of the photographic image. This is why no theory of photography, no matter the type, can simply be transposed onto film. Even if the thesis of a "transparency" of the photographic image were correct, it would not, by a long stretch, apply to the status of the filmic image. The visual (and sonic) movement of the image gives rise to a total difference. The world of the feature film is not equivalent to the world of photography.

This is true even and precisely when a film foregrounds the photographic potential of its medium. This is the case in the scene from *Perpetuum Mobile* described at the beginning of chapter 3. For nearly two minutes, as I have noted, Nicolás Pereda's film approaches the style of a photorealist painting. Such paintings are not content with the mere reproduction of the photographic gaze—they explore, transform, and thematize it. Something similar occurs in *Perpetuum Mobile*. One has only to compare a still from this passage with the film sequence itself. The still is a photographic image. What does it show? A young man and an older woman sitting lethargically on a sofa. Where do the persons in the photograph direct their gaze? They look past the camera that recorded this scene. But what do we see in the corresponding point in the film sequence? We see Teresa and Gabino sitting on the sofa, waiting. We recognize two figures about whose life circumstances we already know a great deal from the preceding narrative. Where do the two of them direct their gaze within the film sequence? They *do not* look past the camera, for within the fiction of this film and most other feature films, the camera is nonexistent. To say that they "look past the camera," which of course the *actors* do, is to make an analytical statement *about* the film. Statements of this sort, which I have made again and again in my descriptions of films, underscore the particular nature of the staging in each case. The characters in the scene of the feature film, however, do not look at the film set—with the camera, the director, the technicians, and so on—where the film is created. They gaze into the space of their apartment, where they are waiting for an absent son and brother. The outside of the visible filmic space is entirely different from that of each individual, isolable photographic shot from the sequence. The former lies in the invisible horizon of the world of this film, which is mapped out by its total choreography. This world arises from a visual (and sonic) movement that is generated through the projection of photographic images. This, however, in no way binds this movement to the realistic *gestus* of the photographic image, since a film's imagination can distance itself at will from the claim and the promise of the photographic image.

Of course, an exaggerated film-theoretical realism can, with reference to the photographic nature of traditional films at least, attempt to save itself by means of an additional thesis. Here we come to a third fallacy, a *temporal* fallacy: as an essentially photographic image, film shares the character of being the bringing into presence of a past event. Yet this notion misapprehends the categorical difference, demonstrated in chapters 3 and 5 above, between the temporal form of the photographic image, on one hand, and the filmic image, on the other. Unlike photography, which presents a past present, the cinematic film, even when it deals with past events, takes place in the present tense of its sound and image performance.

Exposing the errors of a film-theoretical realism that is too closely oriented to photography can occasionally lead to an initial, relatively innocuous illusionistic conclusion. In that case, we arrive at the fallacy of a *perceptual* illusionism: because the mobility of the filmic image is made possible by a succession of still images, film is an illusionistic medium. Here it is assumed that in perceiving films we are subject to a fundamental optical illusion. In an optical illusion, something appears to our senses as something that does not, in actuality, correspond to the respective object of our perception. Its appearance diverges from its makeup. In stubborn cases like the Müller-Lyer illusion, the visual impression of two lines of different lengths persists even when we know that both lines have the same length. According to perceptual illusionism, it is same with the perception of films. After all, we know, but cannot see, that the movements on the screen are evoked by a series of distinct, still images.

That is correct, but it has nothing to do with illusion. When we perceive moving pictures, we see a movement of lines, surfaces, or colors that is actually taking place on the screen. Descriptions of what happens on the screen are plainly capable of communicating the truth—they report, correctly or incorrectly, on what plays out before our eyes. A film's play of visual appearances is real, without a doubt. The fact that the technical *cause* of image movement is not perceptually accessible does not mean that this *movement* is mere semblance. The fact that we *cannot* see something (the distinct photographic shots that are the technical cause of the moving image) does not mean that we see something *different* than what is really there. We merely see a different pictorial appearing than would be accessible to us at the cutting table—which is hardly surprising, since artworks are by nature appearances.

Much more serious is—fifth—the fallacy of an *aesthetic* illusionism. It aims directly at the heart of the debate about art and the cinema. Because film, so the reasoning goes, *unlike* photography, does not primarily present something that *has been*, but presents above all the *being-there*[11] of what occurs within it, it is a constitutively illusionistic medium. We experience an occurrence on the cinema screen—inevitably—*as if* it were real. This thesis at least makes the attraction of an illusionistic aesthetics of the cinema understandable. In its first step, it draws an undeniably positive conclusion from a rejection of the temporal fallacy to which competing theories subscribe. To the version of realist philosophies of film informed by time theory, it opposes a version of illusionism informed by time theory. The latter is likewise predisposed to a presentist interpretation of the presentations of feature films. In this it can draw support from determinations that play a key role in this book as well. It interprets them differently than is here the case, however. Narrative and fictional cinema in particular, the illusionist tells us, is an art form that grants its spectators an incomparable form of involvement in its stories. The virtual space of the cinema, intertwined with the real space of the audience via the sound dimension, constitutes the fundamental as-if of this medium, which is presupposed even when it is breached in films by Godard and his ilk. Even if most illusionists are prepared to concede that there are significant nonillusionist *films*, the basic *potential* of the feature film, as they see it, lies in its ability to make the audience believe—if not from beginning to end, at least intermittently—that it is present at a real event.

Indeed, the spectators have been present at a real event, one, moreover, that relates in an exploratory way to real or unreal human circumstances. But it is the real event of the film itself that captivates viewers with its spectacles. Although he or she may invoke it emphatically, the illusionist fails to recognize the particular nature of the cinematic present, being captive to a dogma that works its mischief in the theory of the other performing arts as well. This dogma states that any form of "medium awareness" has a detrimental effect on the intensity of aesthetic experience. Yet even and precisely in cinema, the opposite is the case: a sensorium for the manner in which a filmic narrative is staged does not result in the diminution of aesthetic experience, but in its intensification. The attraction of a filmic story arises from the attraction of its narration and thus enables an attentiveness to both. That is the central aspect of cinema's imaginative disposition, which illusionistic theories can only fail to capture.

Twofold Attention

This fundamental formal characteristic of the cinematic film has been a leitmotif of my observations from the beginning. On one hand, film shares this characteristic with many other art forms; on the other, film lends it a particular articulation that we do not find in any of the other arts. The dramatization of the duality of presentation and that which is presented is the basis of many types of artistic performance. Attentiveness to this tension is the condition of its unreduced perception. In chapter 3, in a discussion of image theory, I introduced the theorem of "twofold attention," with reference to Richard Wollheim, Gottfried Boehm, and Max Imdahl. It reflects the achievement of the artistic image above all in opening a view on that which is presented in or by it within the very configurations of its appearing. What we recognize as being presented in or by an image springs from the relations of this presented view. Relations of this nature played a central role already in this book's first two chapters. The "architecture" of a film arises from the dynamics of a *space that occurs* along with everything that occurs *within that space*. The "music" of a film takes place as movement *within* the image and at the same time as movement *of* the image. The true "spectacle" of a feature film, as chapter 4 went on to suggest, emerges from an interaction between the dimensions of attraction and narration, in which often neither dominates the other. Moreover, filmic narration unfolds within a structural tension between narrating and narrated perspectives (and often a plurality of such perspectives). In all of this, the temporal form of cinema plays a crucial role. The spectators of a feature film participate in an eminent way in whatever is presented because they are involved in an eminent way in the present of its presentation.

The possibility of twofold attention in the senses noted above is always available in the cinema. This possibility is inherent in film's imaginative constitution as a difference between what is presented and its presentation—and in the various facets of this difference that I have just enumerated. The fact that simultaneous attention to the event of the film and the events in the film is always *possible* does not mean, however, that it is always *necessary* in order to be captivated by a film. To voice this reservation is not to play into the hands of the illusionist. It is merely to underscore that the possibilities in question can be realized in different ways, in a film's organization as well as in its perception. Some films—like *In the Mood for Love*—demand twofold attention simply in order to be appreciated; some—like *The Searchers, Zabriskie Point,* or *The Bourne Supremacy*—only suggest it, but all films allow it, for the simple reason that films are *made of* these doublings.

This constitutive makeup of films opens up a spectrum of possibilities for their perception, which viewers can make use of in various ways, regardless of how much or how little a film seems to suggest one possibility or the other. Viewers can attend *simultaneously* to the filmic narrative and to the nature of its dramaturgy of sound and image; they can let their attention *oscillate* between the two poles; or they can *shift* from one perspective to the other in the course of viewing. Often viewers will linger *more* in one or the other of these modes of attention. It is also possible for viewers to place their focus principally on the narrated story or on the manner of its staging. What is not possible, however, while following a film, is to pay no attention whatsoever to one or the other of these dimensions. To do so would mean to shut one's eyes and ears to the film. Even viewers who attempt to concentrate exclusively on the *makeup* of the film will be unable to ignore its *story*, since it is, after all, the story that is unfolding in this particular manner of staging. Even viewers who allow themselves to be spellbound by the *story* of a film are, in so doing, allowing themselves to be drawn in by the *film*, that is, by the ways in which it is realized in the calculations of its form. Certainly, a film can be viewed with vastly different forms and degrees of *awareness* of the subtleties of its presentation. These are always *in play*, however, as even the illusionist would readily acknowledge. Yet more than this, they are part of the audience's play *of attention*, in different forms and degrees, from the moment it engages with the filmic events. The audience engages with the events of a performance that has no need to disguise its character as a performance, but rather, by virtue of its presence, makes it possible to accomplish the occasional miracles of its presentations.

This concurrent "medium awareness," which involvement in filmic events always tolerates and often enough demands, should not be equated with an elaborated reflection on a film's operation; the latter is only sometimes needed in order to be moved by a film. Nor does it have to imply an expressly interpretive effort, for which many films leave their audiences no time. It can consist merely in a fascination with the style of a film's direction, an appreciation for the composition of situations and sequences, or even in annoyance about a film's uninspired construction. Immersion and absorption in the cinema, then, must not be understood in a one-dimensional fashion. Being spellbound by a film results, at a basic level, from going along with the tensions of the film's progression, which arise through its handling of space and time, the interaction of its perspectives, and the interpenetration of attraction and narration.

Illusion as a Technique

Resonance with the audience always comes down to this multidimensional appearing. Admittedly, it is not without its pitfalls. Halfway through Alfred Hitchcock's *The Birds* (USA, 1963), the elegant Melanie Daniels (Tippi Hedren) sits waiting on a bench next to an elementary school; we hear a repetitive children's song coming from inside. Behind her we see a climbing structure, vacant at first, onto which a crow lands. In a close-up, we see Daniels light a cigarette. Cut. View of the climbing structure on which four crows are now perched. Cut. We see the woman smoking. Cut. Another crow lands on the structure. Cut. Daniels, smoking. Cut. Two more crows fly up. Longer close-up shot of Daniels, who looks around, without noticing anything of what is happening behind her, and finally looks up. Cut. View of blue sky; a pan follows the flight of a crow. Cut. Close-up of Daniels, who follows the bird's flight, slowly turning around. Cut. A pan watches the flight of the crow, which lands on the climbing structure, now thick with crows; more crows are lined up on the rooftops of two buildings as well as a wall in the background. Cut. Shot of the climbing structure, crowded with birds. Cut. Daniels in suppressed panic.

The structure filled with crows prepared for aggression (as both the character and the audience suspect and will soon know for certain) is only seen for five seconds. There is a reason for this. In the brief moments in which we catch sight of it, the assembly of birds on the structure appears as if all of its members were living creatures. But this impression is deceptive. Looking at the scene analytically, one notes that only a few of the creatures are moving; the others are stuffed. Even watching the film in real time, one can see this, though it is hardly noticeable at first viewing. (What one cannot see: the birds lined up on the roof in the background of the image are held in place by magnets.) Here an illusionistic effect is produced of the sort that is common enough in feature films. Something seems to be something and thus looks like something that it is really not. This process must be understood correctly, however. It has nothing to do with a constitutively illusionistic character of feature films. Here too, semblance is in the service of films' appearing.[12] The as-if of an occasional illusionistic technique always depends upon a just-as of the unfolding of filmic space and filmic time.

These sleights of hand achieve their significance from their contribution to the construction of particular sequences and thus to that of the respective film as a whole. The apparency that they engender can only brought forth in the already-established world of a film. This world must already exist before the wool can be pulled over the spectators' eyes and ears. Techniques like those deployed in the scene from *The Birds* support the fiction of the film (in this case, that of an extremely aggressive bird population). The realization of this fiction with the aid of an illusionistic visual impression does not lend the film itself an illusionistic character. That techniques such as this provide no grounds for extrapolating illusion from fiction (this would simply be yet another fallacy) is evident from the fact that we can become fully aware of them without our interest in the respective scenes diminishing in the slightest. On the contrary, this awareness often heightens the attraction of a film for its viewers.

This is also the case with the highly artificial car chase from *The Bourne Supremacy* described in chapter 2. Like many other action scenes in the cinema, it never took place anywhere. No such series of collisions ever occurred on the streets of Moscow. No car chase that could have occurred there could ever have played out with such visual and acoustic musicality. The episode in the film is constructed, through and through, from a montage of images and sounds. It takes place only here, in the film's imagination. It does not draw its attraction from an illusion; rather, it draws its intensity from the attraction of its sonic and visual appearing.

Caché

One does not have to particularly appreciate the considerable technical sophistication of a film like *The Bourne Supremacy* to be captivated by it. There are films, however, that not only permit or suggest a multifaceted attention to the tension between aesthetic attraction and fictional narration, as well as to the heterogeneity of their perspectives—but practically force such attention. In Michael Haneke's film *Caché* (France et al., 2005), filmic images are what shake up the order of a well-situated bourgeois life and that of the film's own fiction at the same time. The film begins with a long take of a house in an upscale Paris neighborhood, shot from an alley with a static camera. For a full minute and a half, the opening credits form against the background of this image, after which the image remains for an additional thirty-four seconds without comment. The sounds of the outdoors are audible, a few passersby move through the image, among them a woman who exits the house toward which the camera's gaze is directed. After more than two minutes, we hear the dialogue of a man and a woman discussing something that is puzzling them. After barely three minutes, the first cut takes place. We see a man come out of the house, followed by a woman (the same woman we saw before); the man looks around and goes back in the house. Next, the shot from the beginning appears again, and the dialogue between the two characters resumes—and then, after almost four minutes, the image suddenly moves, in a slow forward motion, so that we now realize what we are seeing is not an inner-filmic objective shot of the house at all, but rather a video recording that is being played *in* the house. The image that the audience has been looking at for several minutes is the object that has thrown the two viewers within the film into confusion. After that, the video is stopped, rewound, and played again, while the pair attempts to analyze the image, though without success. Only after about five minutes does the film narrative enter the house that was the object of the observing images from the beginning of the film. We see the man and the woman standing in their living room in front of the television on which they are watching the video that previously filled the screen. In their private space, they are confronted with a gaze from the outside, one that they are not able to situate in the world of their lives.

Again and again, Georges Laurent (Daniel Auteuil), a television moderator, receives videotapes of this kind; despite every research effort, their origins remain inexplicable to him and his wife, Anne (Juliette Binoche), a publisher, throughout the film. Neither do the film's viewers receive any explanation. Yet little by little, it becomes apparent that the tapes refer to a shameful incident from Laurent's childhood, one that he has repressed. (He saw to it that a boy of Algerian origins, taken in by his parents, was cast out of the family; the boy's own parents, it is implied, were murdered by French police in the 1961 massacre in Paris.) In this way—mounting over the course of the film and later coming to a grisly crisis—*Caché* orchestrates a disintegration of the main character's images of himself and his life, and at the same time of the images through which the film speaks of the state of individual and societal concealment and repression. The main character conceals the memory of a traumatic experience; the polite society to which he belongs conceals the social indifference from which it profits; the film conceals the origins of the video recordings that it makes a catalyst of its narrative.

Within the narrative of *Caché*, the standpoint from which the videos are recorded remains consistently mysterious. In the reality of the fiction, from beginning to end, they establish a gaze from nowhere. This creates a lasting uncertainty, not only on the part of the characters in the film, but also on the part of the spectators. When shots and scenes change, it remains unclear to the viewer whether particular sequences are presenting the perspective of the enigmatic external images, that of the participating characters, or that of objective views within the world of the film. The longer the film continues, the more the audience begins to doubt whether the sequence it is watching is located in the world of the film or represents the ominous gaze from outside. In most cases, the status of the previous sequence is revealed as the story progresses. But in another passage, it is possible *simultaneously* to construe a traveling shot taken from a car as an external image and as a perspective that is immanent to the narrated world. This game of confusion that the film plays with the status of its own perspectives contains elements of an illusionistic operation. Yet, again, this operation only gains its function from the establishment of a filmic world inside of which a difference between subjective and objective, internal and external, perspectives can even arise. The structure of the film acquiesces to deception and—in part—lays it bare again in order to point to what is possibly deceptive about its own images: this is how its imagination proceeds.

Herein lies a radical difference with the logic of the shots in a film like *North by Northwest*, in which the observer always knows the standpoint from which the particular events are presented. *Caché*, in contrast, stages structurally tainted views of its story's settings. The anonymous shots move the viewer partly into the position of the characters who are also trying to understand what these recordings mean. Yet a severe asymmetry remains. For while the characters find themselves subjected to a tainted view of their own lives, the film's viewers are confronted with a tainted view of the characters' lives—and at the same time with views that are incommensurable with the narrative construction of the film itself. The participation in the perspective of the characters, the assimilation of a perspective on the characters, and the bringing into presence of the film's own perspectivity: all of this must occur simultaneously, because *Caché* admits one only by imposing the remainder on its audience. In watching a film like this one, it is not only possible to direct one's attention to both the narrated events and the event of the narration—it is utterly impossible to watch it any other way.

Film as Emotion

The End, Yet Again

In the last three minutes or so of John Ford's *The Searchers*, an extreme change of mood occurs. During an attack on the Comanche camp, accompanied by dramatic orchestral music, Ethan Edwards rides on horseback out of the tepee of Chief Scar, whom Martin Pawley has previously shot. He holds Scar's bloody scalp in his hand. Ethan's darkened gaze falls on his niece Debbie, who is fleeing from the camp. Ethan follows her. Martin Pawley, who fears for his stepsister's life, attempts to stop him. Ethan strikes him with his revolver and resumes his pursuit of Debbie. At a distance, from the inside of a cave, we see Debbie running down a dusty slope, pursued by Ethan at a gallop. Debbie throws herself to the ground at the mouth of the cave. Ethan stops and dismounts. Martin comes running up and draws his revolver. Ethan bends down and lifts Debbie up. The dramatic music is replaced by the elegiac title melody. Debbie puts her arms around Ethan's neck. The music goes silent. Change of scene: surrounded by his comrades in arms, the Reverend Captain Samuel Johnson Clayton (Ward Bond) is having a bullet removed from his backside. There is an embarrassing encounter with the colonel of the cavalry that has arrived too late. The title melody begins again during a cross-fade to a side view of the Jorgensen family house. Hired hand Mose Harper (Hank Worden) sits in a rocking chair in the foreground. The Jorgensens come out of the house and gaze into the distance. A group of riders is approaching, among them Martin Pawley and Ethan Edwards with Debbie. Laurie Jorgensen rushes to her fiancé. The old Jorgensens look on, visibly moved, as Ethan Edwards lifts Debbie from his horse. At this moment, the orchestral title melody is replaced by the sentimental Western song familiar from the opening credits. Close-up of Mose Harper blissfully rocking in his chair. Ethan carries Debbie up to the edge of the front porch and hands her over to the custody of her foster parents. The three move slowly into the interior of the house. Ethan pauses, hesitating. He steps to the side to let the young couple pass, then looks inside the house, but finally turns away and walks off at a sauntering gait. The world of the film closes as the end of the Western song is followed by dramatic orchestral music.

The desecration of a corpse, a threat of murder, the puzzling turn-around, the comic intermezzo, the happy homecoming, the repetition of the opening scene in reverse, the exclusion of the hero from the sphere to which he has restored peace, together with the divergent musical instrumentation of this rapid succession of changes: I cannot watch the finale of *The Searchers*, even after the thirtieth time, whether in the cinema or on the computer, without being touched by it. Each time I am close to tears. The scene moves me, it transports me, it elicits reactions from me against which I am nearly defenseless.

The Illusionist's Final Appearance

This confession calls forth the illusionist again. "That," he proclaims, "is what the cinema is all about: letting oneself be moved by the movements of a filmic narrative! We want to participate in a narrative event that allows us to experience its progression with feeling!"

When he's right, he's right. To be sure, not all spectators will respond as I do to the end of *The Searchers*, but all will be able to think of films that

have carried them away at the end, not unlike this one still does to me. At
the end of *Bringing up Baby*, they laugh about the collapse of a giant dino-
saur skeleton, which undoes the ossified life of Dr. David Huxley as well,
once and for all. At the end of *North by Northwest*, they thrill to one of
the most famous match cuts in film history as Roger Thornhill, with one
hand, pulls the not-insubstantial Eve Kendall up from the precipice at
Mount Rushmore, only to hoist her into the upper bunk of a sleeping car,
whereupon the train drives into a tunnel. At the end of *Zabriskie Point*,
after the long explosion sequence has come to an abrupt end, the viewers drive with the young heroine into a glowing sunset, which might be a
source of comfort were the trip not accompanied by an ironic swan song.
In the closing scene of *Apocalypse Now*, viewers are transfixed by the
gaze of the main character, staring into the void of the night, a stare that
corresponds to the one with which the film began; only now the viewers
themselves are captive in the oppressive daydream.

Some films, however, are expressly created to stir the emotions of the
audience in their finale precisely by soothing the agitations to which it
has previously been subjected. At the end of *The Lord of the Rings: The
Return of the King* (Peter Jackson, USA, NZ, 2003), before a melancholic
epilogue, there is a three-stage emotional coda. After nearly three hours of
the film, it extends over five minutes in a temporal stretch. With a majestic
gesture and accompanied by swelling orchestral music, the camera travels
up a gigantic, wedge-shaped rock ledge that towers over the land, atop
which, following their victory over the dark forces, the surviving fighters
have assembled in tremendous numbers. In the forecourt of the castle, a
new king is being crowned. Solemn words are spoken. Rejoicing breaks
out. The king intones an exotic chant; its sound accompanies the second
phase of the ceremony. The king walks through the ranks of his faithful
and his companions, to whom he is bidding farewell. Behind a silk ban-
ner, he is astonished to discover his true love. Emotional, ardent embrace.
Applause from the onlookers. The orchestral music sets in again. Together
the couple continues on the path until they are standing before four hobbits. When the latter want to bow down before the king, he stops them.
Now the third stage of emotional direction is launched. Even viewers who
have kept their cool up to this point may now be laid low. "My friends,"
the king declares to his companions, "you bow to no one." *He* bows before them—and with him, so do all the hardened warriors. A long shot

makes visible the motion of the kneeling crowd, which the little hobbits now tower above. From a low angle, the camera moves to the stunned faces of the four figures, before it zooms out for a distance shot of the scene from a great height.

Of course it is not only—and sometimes not so much at all—at the end where a film's movement can especially move the audience emotionally. Yet in many films, the entire dynamic culminates in the gestures of their final sequence. The illusionist sees this no differently. But he insists that a feature film cannot draw its absorbing energy from a constant emphasis on the sleights of hand of its own staging. He considers any such instances as an exception that must not be raised to the level of a paradigmatic case. The tears that we shed in the cinema, the fear that grips us, the joy and *schadenfreude* that come over us, and all the other fluctuations of sensing and feeling that films let us live through: all of this, the illusionist believes, is only explicable because we comprehend the occurrences in a film as if they were not merely the occurrence of a representation. This, however, is precisely the reason he misconstrues the particular emotionality of the cinematic experience. He has no faith in the emotionality of the film itself. Even and precisely the affects that a feature film *awakens* in its audience arise from the emotions that it *plays* with via its performance. From beginning to end they are the product of the film's imaginative disposition.

Motion and Emotion

In the multiplicity of cultural practices of agitation and animation, going to the cinema by no means stands alone. With an evidently autobiographical accent, Immanuel Kant, in his *Anthropology from a Pragmatic Point of View*, asks: "Why is a game (especially for money) so attractive and, if it is not too selfish, the best distraction and relaxation after a long intellectual exertion, since through idleness one recuperates only slowly?" The answer is "Because a game is a state of incessant movement between fearing and hoping."[1] Kant points out laconically that a dialectic of movement and being-moved characterizes every form of game or playing. This is by no means limited to the arts, but it is in effect there as well: "By what means are *plays* (whether tragedies of comedies) so alluring? Because in all of them certain difficulties enter in—anxiety and confusion between hope and joy—and so the play of opposing affects by the conclusion of the piece advances the life of the spectator, since it has stirred up motion within him."[2] "Motion" is the key term here. Theater, too (and we would add cinema from our contemporary standpoint), sets off a process of "incessant movement between fearing and hoping," as Kant describes the participation—be it passive or active—in the practices of game playing.

Kant is always aware that this interplay—and often enough, this fusion—of positive and negative expectations represents a basic tension of human life in general. Yet for him, the point of playful "occupations" lies precisely in the fact that, for the limited duration it takes to carry them out, those who indulge in them attain a distance from the seriousness of the various other affairs of their lives, a seriousness that is not time-limited, or at least not to anywhere near the same extent. The significance of play derives from a bodily or psychic agitation that is undergone for its own sake, from an ambivalent state of being-moved that can be enjoyed precisely in its ambivalence. Many sorts of games and ways of playing allow their participants to endure fluctuations of luck and success that in other contexts they could never countenance to the same degree, if at all.

Admittedly, the distinction between games in general and the games of art is not explicitly noted in Kant's anthropology of the game. This distinction must be figured in if we wish to bring into view the particularity of the emotions involved in art's games. With the arts, there is the additional factor that the "motion" of those participating in these games is aroused by various forms of the *performance* of emotion and movement. Each of the arts has its own possibilities at its disposal for animating its audience. For the aesthetics of the cinema, this raises the question of how *its* motion is or, rather, can be connected to *our* emotion.

Corporeality

This question has accompanied us from the beginning. Each of the preceding chapters, in its way, has already given an answer. It is the spatial, temporal, pictorial, narrative, exploratory, and imaginative form of the filmic process that enables a particular form of emotional investment in the film's presentation. It absorbs the sensuous and the psychic attention of the viewer to a heightened degree compared to the other arts.

In the cinema, the spectators move as aesthetic subjects, seeing and hearing, within a virtual world that is beyond their bodily grasp, and let themselves be moved—seeing and hearing, feeling and understanding—by what occurs *in that world* and how *that world itself* occurs.

The fact that, in the cinema, we linger as "aesthetic subjects" in a space and a time that are "beyond our bodily grasp" certainly in no way means that we are not affected as bodily subjects while we are there. On the contrary: as corporeal beings, we find ourselves, in the space of the cinema, transposed in a superlative way into the sphere of the aesthetic process. The situation of perception here differs in a significant way from the observation of other modes of the artistic image. We do not stand before an image that confronts us with its unique point of view; we stand in a visual river that reaches, by means of its sound, into the real space where we linger. As at a musical performance, but even more intensely because of the eye's surrender to the visual events, the body of the spectator functions, in the cinema, as a resonating body for a range of visual and auditory impulses that are also linked synaesthetically to the other senses.[3]

Shortly before *North by Northwest*, with a spectacular match cut, provides its two main characters an opportunity for marital relations, Eve Kendall is dangling over a dark precipice with only Roger Thornhill's right hand, which holds tight to her left one, preventing a deadly fall. Thornhill clings desperately with his left hand to the edge of a cliff. He pleads for help from the spy who is watching the scene. The latter hesitates, then moves toward the ledge. The camera travels in the direction of the cliff until we see Thornhill's hand in the center of the image. The villain's shoe moves closer to the unprotected and defenseless hand, finally resting on it fully. In a long shot, we see how the scoundrel increases the pressure on his victim's hand with sadistic slowness. A spectator does not have to imagine that it is *his* hand that is being abused and certainly not that *he* is hanging above an abyss with a blonde on his arm. After all, there he sits, undisturbed in his seat, and if he is accompanied by a companion, she is there next to him. But spectators also have hands, and they are aware of their vulnerability. It is this bodily awareness that is activated in the film's spectators by this shot. In watching the scene, they can trace how it would feel to be subjected to the physical harassment that is depicted in the image. Because of this experience of feeling, they share in the drama of this scene, which has not the slightest concern with realistic representation.

The cinema of suspense frequently operates with techniques of this sort. In the finale of *True Lies*, we see Harry Tasker's daughter, who has been abducted by a terrorist, fleeing from her pursuer on a crane high above the city. Spectators with even a trace of a fear of heights will go weak in the knees at this episode—but not because they *imagine* that they are the ones clamoring around up there, but rather because they are following the filmic *representation* of this action with considerable unease. Effects such as this that stir up bodily sensations are by no means limited to the cinema of suspense. A gripping scene in Michael Haneke's *Amour* (France, Germany, Austria, 2012) is a case in point. Georges (Jean-Louis Trintignant) attempts to give his wife, Anne (Emmanuelle Riva), frail and suffering from dementia after a stroke, something to drink from a feeding cup. She does not want to drink. With a fixed gaze, Anne tightly closes her lips. Georges coaxes her, pleads with her, and finally tries to force her to drink. Anne remains stubborn. The liquid runs down her chin and drips onto her nightgown. Georges picks up a towel and wipes her mouth and neck. Viewers who are familiar with situations of this sort, when faced with this scene, will not merely remember their own devotion, their own coaxing, and their own helplessness; the sequence of motions in the image will in fact awaken a bodily memory of a physical and psychic demand with which they are intimately acquainted. It is in this state of affective commotion that they take in what is represented in this scene of the film.

The membrane of the spectator's sensitive and susceptive body is set vibrating in countless ways. Each plot twist, each change of mood, each lag or acceleration, and any other surprise held in store, to be introduced suddenly or gradually over the course of a feature film, affects the body-based sensuous and psychic balance of its audience: irritates it, attacks it, churns it, and sometimes restores it to some degree. Those shocking images of cinema that are burned into the memory of its spectators represent an extreme form of this cinematic agitation: the shower scene in *Psycho* (Alfred Hitchcock, USA, 1960), the scene in *The Godfather* (Francis Ford Coppola, USA, 1972) in which a man awakes in bed with a bloody horse head under the blanket, or the scene in *Caché*, in which, without warning, the character of Majid (Maurice Bénichou) slits his own throat with a kitchen knife in front of Georges Laurent. Yet moments such as this are only a counterpole to the quieter means by which films like *La Notte*

(Michelangelo Antonioni, Italy, France, 1961), *Fontane Effi Briest*, *Taste of Cherry*, or *Amour* get under their audience's skin.

Sensate Understanding

At this juncture, however, our entire project would go awry if we were to reduce the power of the cinema to the purely emotional effect of its films. Not only would the cause of these effects sink into oblivion, the effects themselves would be misrepresented—and along with them the entire relationship of the spectators to the presence of a film. The particular film is not merely the cause, the impetus, or the trigger of the audience's emotions, but rather the *object* of these emotions. The audience's affective reactions are an elemental form of the *comprehension* of the film's composition.

"Sensations," "feelings," and "moods" often take on crucial significance here. Sensations like pain, nausea, or vertigo are physical conditions that can be triggered in numerous ways. Feelings like love, hatred, fear, or admiration are spontaneous forms of evaluative assessment of particular objects or situations. Moods like euphoria or depression, on the other hand, give expression to a momentary or lasting perspective on one's own life circumstances. For our purposes it is not necessary to untangle the delicate relations between these types of emotionality. To be sure, not all of these forms of affective awareness are "intentional states" that would include a characterization of an object. Yet in their interconnectedness with the positions taken by feelings, nonintentional sensations and relatively indeterminate moods attain an unequivocal focus during the cinema experience: they too are directed toward the film that they accompany on its course. The various ways of being emotionally affected bleed into one another and thus color the audience's attention to the cinematic process.

In any case, the emotions involved in the perception of a film must not be considered in isolation from the cognitive, imaginative, and associative components of its assimilation. In the cinema, as in the other arts, emotional receptivity to a particular work forms an integral part of the capacity for assimilating its presentation. This is hardly surprising, since emotions are basic forms of positive and negative attunement to situations of all sorts. They are not the adversary of considered and reflective action, but rather an indispensable compass in the attempt to lead a halfway honorable existence. Without emotions, we would have no sense whatsoever of true and false, good and bad, and all the other ambivalences of life. Nothing would matter to us. The intellectual economy of the human being cannot be separated from the spectrum of human passions.

These constellations are activated by all the arts in different ways. The cinema too, after its fashion, plays through the possibilities of human experience, often in an exemplary sense. In the *dispositif* of its singular form of movement, it captivates the audience emotionally to a remarkable degree. Being taken along in this way represents the mode of taking-in in which films come to be perceived in the cinema. Films enable and demand a sensate understanding capable of keeping pace with the progression of a filmic narrative.[4] For the most part, keeping pace has little to do with the subtle deciphering of filmic composition. It happens as the course of events is assimilated, in the dark of the cinema, by seeing, hearing, and feeling, with reactions of laughing and crying, fright and surprise, playing a considerable role. This going along relates to the apparatus of the films to which it addresses itself; it assimilates them and makes sense of them. A film is far more than a mere instrument for evoking feelings; feeling aroused by a film is far more than just a reaction to its presentation. Films and emotions are made for each other because the latter are answers to that with which the former address their audience.[5]

For the theory of cinema, this means that we do not understand the motive force of the cinematic experience if we do not understand the movement of film. This is the starting point for everything to do with a film's composition, its imagination, its expressivity. Only if, only because, and only as long as we take a responsive attitude toward a film can we come into resonance with its vibration. It is the nature of a film's expressivity that gives rise to the nature of the emotionality of our perception of it.[6]

Expressivity

"Anybody got a match?" asks Lauren Bacall in the role of Marie Browning in a legendary scene from the film *To Have and Have Not* (Howard Hawks, USA, 1944). In a relaxed stance, she leans on the frame of the open door to the modest hotel room rented by Humphrey Bogart, alias

Harry Morgan—it is the first contact with the man to whom she will later play much more than just a supporting role. She strikes a pose that makes her irresistible to someone like Harry Morgan, even if it is against his will at first. The character visible in this shot appears both unapproachable and alluring, both self-assured and vulnerable, and as beautiful as she is inscrutable. This is how the *actress* portrays the character, this is how *the character* portrays herself—and this is how the *film* portrays her, by providing her her first appearance in bright illumination broken up by diagonally falling shadows.

Fritz Lang's first sound film, *M* (Germany, 1931), unlike a number of his earlier works, is not an expressionist film. In many segments it verges on a variety of social realism as well as an early form of police procedural. Yet there is a key sequence that is indebted to an expressionist aesthetic. Figures of the city's criminal underworld, seeing their operations jeopardized by the frantic activities of the police, track down the child murderer Hans Beckert (Peter Lorre), whom the latter are seeking to no avail. The criminals bring Beckert to a dark cellar vault where they intend to put him on trial. After some back and forth, the "accused" is given the opportunity to testify. In the most famous scene of his acting career, Peter Lorre gives a nearly five-minute monologue describing the torments of the sex offender that he embodies. In a pathos-laden outburst accompanied by fervent facial expressions and gesticulations, Beckert tells of the impulses of which he feels he is at the mercy. In a play of light and dark that sculpts the soft face of the actor, multiple levels of expression intersect here as well: the actor's brilliant performance, the plasticity that his character attains in this moment, and the direction that, in the darkness of the scene, isolates him for a short while as if on the theatrical stage.

But in cinema even extreme emotions can be presented with extraordinary coolness—which in fact lends them a particular salience. In the film *Fox and His Friends* (*Faustrecht der Freiheit*; West Germany, 1975) by Rainer Werner Fassbinder, the director himself plays the character of the unemployed actor Franz Biberkopf, known as "Fox the Talking Head," who is thoroughly fleeced by his gay friends after winning a considerable sum in the lottery. Toward the end of the film, Biberkopf is sitting alone in the dark in the flashy sports car that he has managed to hold onto as a last refuge. He turns on the radio, which plays Leonard Cohen's deeply sad song "Bird on the Wire." Cut. The camera switches from the interior of the car to the outside. Through the windshield we watch as Biberkopf lights a cigarette and stares, almost motionless, into nothingness. With a slight movement he activates the windshield wiper, which twice sweeps back and forth over the dry glass. A last gesture of tenderness, the wiping away of tears, which the hero is no longer able to cry, is replaced with an automatic movement.

Regardless of the degree to which a feature film may be "expressive" or even "expressionistic" with respect to style, various dimensions of expressivity always shape its presentation. What is more, expressive phenomena in the cinema are not only tied to the presence of the human body. Objects, spaces, and landscapes can also have and show expression in any number of ways. Neither the expressivity nor the emotionality of a film sequence or a film in its entirety is exclusively bound to the representation of its characters' emotions. Yet each of these aspects always remains bound to the audiovisual motion of a film in the totality of its staging: bound to the nature of the imagination with which the film fashions its narrative. All "motion" on the spectators' part emerges from this imaginative constitution of the film as it unfolds; it is always oriented toward this constitution. That, again, is the reason that the emotions that carry the viewing of a film cannot be understood merely as an effect of its dramaturgy. After all, they give access to the form and the content of a film. Spectators, in their sensate involvement, perceive and take in (and in the best case, assimilate) these emotions with which the film attempts to captivate them.

Engagement

The spaces, moods, and atmospheres created in narrative feature films encompass the actions of the characters that carry their stories. They are essentially made for the characterization of these figures. The rhythm of their changes both signals and demonstrates how the characters fare. If a film is to attract an audience's interest, it must succeed in arousing interest in its characters. Their fate has to matter to the spectators. The latter cannot remain indifferent to the characters without being indifferent to the film.

Because the feature film has particular capabilities for tapping into the full complement of its spectators' senses, it can, in a particular way, make the situation of its audience correspond with that of its characters. This correspondence must not, however, be confused with a convergence (construed in an illusionistic sense), as if the spectators would have to place themselves in the characters' situation in their imagination in order to make sense of a film. The emotional situation of the spectators in the cinema never even approaches being the same as *one* of the characters in a film, much less the *many characters* that populate some films. This is due to the structural perspectivity of narration, as discussed at length in chapters 5 and 7. The narrative perspective *on* a character—even if it is only *one*—is never identical to the perspective *of* the character. The point-of-view shots that repeatedly show us what Roger Thornhill sees in the cornfield scene in *North by Northwest* only attain their significance within a presentation that establishes an external perspective on this character and the fictional world in which he moves. It is only because we see him as he does not and cannot see himself that we are engaged, as spectators, with the situation through which his involuntary adventures lead him. What captivates us in the drama of these adventures (and in their comedy) is always at the same time the *view,* presented by the film's staging, on what takes place as they run their course.

With regard to the emotionality of going along with a character and that character's representation, another polarity is also pertinent here. We can feel *with* a character or we can feel *for* him or her (or both at once). We can be happy with or suffer with a character, but we may also harbor feelings for him or her—concern, compassion, shame, or contempt—that the character does not share and would not find appropriate. This is made clear in the scene from *Amour* described above. Its representation opens up the possibility for the spectator to feel with Georges as he cares for Anne and desperately tries to motivate her to drink. After three excruciating minutes, however, the situation escalates. Anne spits out the tea that was forced into her mouth, whereupon George spontaneously slaps her face. Anne's face shows a horrified expression. Georges is shaken and ashamed; he asks Anne to forgive him. This moment of violence briefly pulls spectators out of their participation in Georges's experience, even if they can now feel greater compassion for his helplessness and will soon feel *with him* again. In fact, this instability of empathy for even an exceptionally sympathetic film character is practically the key factor in our absorption with the experiences of the characters in a film. Spectators in the cinema are entertained by "the play of opposing affects," to use Kant's phrase.[7] It arises from a play of the representation of heterogeneous affective situations that confront the audience in an often unpredictable flux.

This is why it is misleading to interpret spectators' going-along with a film as resulting from an "identification" with its main characters. In fact, a spectator's relationship to the cast of a feature film stems from complex and often conflicting forms of engagement:[8] an interest in the fate of a character, or multiple characters, that can be more positive or more negative, but which often includes sympathy and antipathy in combination.[9] We may grow fond of characters that we would avoid in real life; figures we would consider like us in our everyday lives may become suspect. One has only to recall the ambivalent characters that Humphrey Bogart played in many of his classic roles. Figures like Ethan Edwards in *The Searchers*, Colonel Kurtz in *Apocalypse Now,* or Tommy DeVito in *Goodfellas* are of another caliber—men as ambiguous as they are brutal, but who nevertheless exert an extraordinary fascination (partly due to the achievements of the actors portraying them: John Wayne, Marlon Brando, and Joe Pesci). The directing in *United 93* offers an extreme example of the divided emotional states that a film can provoke. In the preliminary scenes inside the airplane that is destined to be hijacked and crashed, the four terrorists are treated no differently in the directing than their soon-to-be victims. This equal treatment has a disconcerting effect. The longer the leader delays in giving the command to seize control of the plane, the more restless his fellow combatants become until, as a spectator, one almost begins to share in the assailants' anxiety. For five minutes, one finds oneself in a state of impatience with regard to both the tactics of the characters and the cadence of the film: one practically wishes for the terrorists to go ahead and strike—feeling, at the same time, the perversity of such a wish.

Yet in whatever combination we may, as spectators, engage with the fate of good and evil characters, heroes and heroines, go-getters and dawdlers, lovers and sufferers, seducers and the seduced, winners and losers, despots and the disenfranchised, the lucky and the unlucky, this much is certain: empathy in the cinema is categorically different from the empathy of which we are capable—or incapable—in "real life." Illusionistic interpretations founder on this point, as well. They can only suggest that we come to tears at the end of *The Searchers* primarily because we let ourselves be convinced that we are actually present as a young woman

(Debbie) is rescued—and that we consequently experience the same (or somehow analogous) feelings as we would in a situation such as this. But that is absurd. In fact, we are touched in an entirely different way by events in the cinema than we could (or even should) be by comparable real-world situations. Not only are we able to distribute our sympathy and antipathy differently; we can also allow these feelings to intensify or diminish, unlike in situations in which we are or could be involved in actuality. In the cinema, we can live out our capacity for experience in a special way because we feel we are encouraged by the form of filmic representation to alter our experience. Film's imaginations afford us a way of feeling through and thinking through the possibilities and impossibilities of being-in-the-world[10] as humans, in a way that is otherwise unavailable in the world.

Twofold Attention, Again

To be sure, the spaces, atmospheres, rhythms, and gestures engendered in the dramaturgy of feature films are essentially made for the characterization of the film's figures, as stated above. Yet we must not lose sight of the fact that the perception of *characters* is always at the same time a perception of their *characterization*—or of the fact that the former is compatible with a full awareness of this interdependency. The changing, often divergent, and sometimes experimental emotional states with which spectators follow the course of a film always relate to the perspective from which a film recounts the fate of its characters. This relationship may be more explicit or more implicit, but it is always present, otherwise the events and the story of a film would never come into their own. On one hand, this means that, in the cinema, sympathy too—and especially sympathy— derives from a twofold attention to both what is presented in a film and the manner of its presentation, although this attention may not be particularly conscious. On the other hand, however, the fact that engagement with a film and its characters *derives from* attention of this sort means that one can attend to both dimensions with full awareness without diminishing the engagement with the film in any way.

It is this second aspect that an illusionistic theory of cinema fails to recognize. The engagement with the characters of a film is in essence an engagement with its composition as *film*. Cinematic experience depends from start to finish on the fact that something is *presented* to us in a particular way *as feelable*. It depends on the fact that we let ourselves be touched by this *presentation* in a way that allows us, in turn, to let ourselves be touched by the fate of the characters (or by various situations and events). Emotional involvement in cinema does not have to, but can at any time, be realized as a twofold fascination: as feeling for the characters entangled in the filmic story and simultaneously as a feeling for the filmic entanglement of the characters and situations. The feeling for the makeup of a film can be, in various ways, in consonance and/or dissonance with the spectators' sympathies and/or antipathies toward the characters, which lends an additional tension to the act of going along with a film. Feature films not only have the potential to arouse feelings that are ambivalent, shifting, or fluctuating in many respects. They can also awaken stereoscopic emotions: emotions that allow us to be caught up in a film while focusing simultaneously on the manner of staging and the fate of the characters.

This is true not only for the scenes from films like *M, To Have and Have Not,* or *Fox and His Friends,* that we have described above; it is true for each of the films called to mind at the start of this chapter and, in fact, for any film that has the power to move its audience. This is not a matter of some particular sophistication unique to auteur cinema; it is a basic disposition of cinema in general. Especially the shocking images with which some films burn themselves into their audiences' memory do not attain their significance by means of mere horror; cinema, after all, is full of horror. Films like *Psycho, The Godfather,* or *Caché* derive their power from the particular formal calculations with which they make their terrors into an event. Running gags are another example. Films that make use of these devices lay bare their own organization. In *Ice Age* and its three sequels, Scrat the saber-toothed squirrel provides comic intermezzi, interrupting and mirroring the action, time and time again. One remembers these appearances and waits for the next one, which draws attention to the contours of the film. Among the many running gags in Ernst Lubitsch's *To Be or Not to Be* there are lines of dialogue, delivered by various speakers in various situations, of this sort: "They named a brandy after Napoleon, they made a herring out of Bismarck, and Hitler is going to end up as a piece of cheese." And: "You know there is always something wrong with a man who doesn't drink, doesn't smoke, doesn't eat meat." Each time, the joke places the speaker in dire straits from which an abject "Heil Hitler" is the only escape.

But breaks of this sort are by no means the only way in which films expose their own makeup. Through the pace with which they lead us through their situations, whether slowed down (as in the cornfield scene in *North by Northwest*) or accelerated (as in the car chase through Moscow in *The Bourne Supremacy*); through the spaces (as in *The Searchers*) that they spectacularly open up and close off; through the perspectives that they thus permit or refuse; through the manner in which they explore their fictional world: films play out their sonic and visual attractions to lend their stories the proper drive.

Mixed Emotions

All of these operations both provoke and color the ways in which we follow a film with our senses and intellect. For this reason, the emotions that move us in the cinema have a particular character. Sometimes more consciously, sometimes more unconsciously, they are focused on what is presented and also on its presentation. Sometimes more consciously, sometimes more unconsciously, they react to the narration and also to the attraction of filmic events. Moreover, they can tolerate relating, with full consciousness, to both at once—in fact, this is often the only way these emotions can come about.

Feelings such as this are not "quasi-emotions"; they are as genuine as emotions can be.[11] Just as we do not merely imagine we are seeing Debbie Edwards, Eve Kendall, Marie Browning, or any other film character, we do not somehow only imagine feeling an emotion for their predicament. Being-moved in the cinema always arises from the fact that, with open eyes, we follow a representation that either fascinates us or leaves us indifferent, because of its qualities as representation: our engagement depends on *what* the occurrences on the screen are presented to us as being and on *how* they are presented.

We do not imagine the corresponding emotions; we have them. We do not imagine experiencing fear for a beleaguered character; we are afraid for her. We do not imagine sharing the character's sorrows; we do share them. We do not merely believe we feel joy for her brief happiness; we are happy along with the character. And so on. Of course, these are entirely different emotions than we would or could feel in real situations in life. But why is this so? It is because these are, in a specific sense, mixed emotions. It is because they arise simultaneously from the drama of a story and the dramaturgy of its narration. It is because they are oriented at once to the success or failure of this representation and to the failure and/or success of the characters that are represented. It is because, in the best cases, we are captivated simultaneously by the trials and tribulations of the characters and the twists and turns of their filmic characterization. It is because, in the cinema, we can wholeheartedly enjoy our tears and our shuddering. It is because even films in which little or nothing joyful takes place elicit our admiration, our enthusiasm, and even our joy. It is because films allow us to affirm the fluctuating emotions with which we follow their presentations in a way that we could not, would not, and would not even wish to do in other spheres of life.

Only the law of the co-presentness of filmic presentation can explain the frequency with which absorption in cinema holds up to repetition. This is the only factor that makes comprehensible why, in the case of many films, the immersive power of cinema does not diminish after multiple, and even frequent viewings, and in fact is often enhanced. Repeated encounters alter the quality of one's attention to the higher rhythm of these films' composition as well as to many details of what is narrated and of the narration itself. Pleasure in the form of the presentation, of whatever is being presented, is heightened. Attending to form in this way is simply a life elixir—and more than that, an aphrodisiac—for being animated by films in the cinema.

Godard

The considerations in this chapter and the previous one render redundant a theory—even a makeshift one—specific to the auteur cinema represented in this book by directors like Antonioni, Fassbinder, Kiarostami, Wong Kar-Wai, and Haneke, among others. Certainly, a film like *First Name: Carmen* (*Prénom Carmen*; Jean-Luc Godard, France, 1983) proceeds in a completely different manner than many of the great films of narrative cinema, regardless of their country of origin or the budget with which they may have been produced. Like others before and after it, this film is an adaptation—though certainly an extremely free one—of Bizet's opera *Carmen*. But telling a story, in this case, is only a secondary point. Godard's film is many things at once: audio drama, music film, landscape film, love story, poetic film, political film, action cinema, as well as a parody of all of these genres—and thus a film that, through its form, poses the question of cinema's form. In one of its dimensions, *First Name: Carmen* is about literal filmmaking (even if, in the film's fiction, the filmmaking is only a sham), but it is also made up of potential films, edited together and overlapping. A refusal to commit to one or a few of the conventional genres, or even to give just a few of them a different twist, characterizes the composition of the entire film.

The title can be understood in the same vein. At the start of the film, we hear the voice of Carmen (Maruschka Detmers) from off screen, declaiming about an unnamed person. She describes this person as "celle qui ne devrait pas s'appeller Carmen" ("the one who should not be named Carmen"). Why should this figure not be named Carmen? The *narrative* of this film provides no answer; it is the film itself that answers the question. The film's name refers less to the erotic unreliability of its heroine than to the aesthetic unreliability of its own attractions. "Je n'ai pas peur, mais c'est parce que je n'ai jamais pu, su, m'attacher" ("I am not afraid, but it is only because I never wanted, never knew how, to become attached"), we hear Carmen's voice say. Precisely this is true of Godard's film, which cannot and does not wish to tie itself down to a particular genre, a particular narrative perspective, a particular mood, much less an unambiguous message. Such cinema, fearless vis-à-vis the conventions of its art, can afford to be, at once, pulp fiction and metafiction, love story and poetology, elegy and parody. It dissolves the bonds that hold its set pieces together in other contexts. It pulls them out of their context and incorporates them into its own. (In that sense, Quentin Tarantino is among Godard's loyal disciples.) The hectic attractionism that holds sway at the high points of every contemporary action film, when its visuals overtake the continuity of its narrative, is inverted in *First Name: Carmen* in a sonic and visual spectacle that collaborates with music and painting in the manner of an installation. This spectacle can dispense with exposition, development, and coda. As in a tonal-surface composition of the New Music, almost all hierarchies are suspended here: between beginning, middle, and end, between image and sound, between narration and reflection. The film is a comedy of metamorphosis of the filmic process that nearly succeeds in squaring the circle: making a film in which all the events *in* the film are only there to refer to the event *of* the film.

The arts of a film like this one take an audience on a different sort of journey than *The Lord of the Rings* and its aesthetic kindred. They play an entirely different game with an audience's expectations. For an audience that is prepared to engage with its choreography, *First Name: Carmen* entertains with a virtuosic combination of comedy and tragedy, contemplation and self-referentiality, repetition and variation. The film takes its audience on an intellectual and emotional roller-coaster ride whose wildness rivals conventional adventure films. If the pole of a captivating narrative recedes in a feature film, the film itself can still captivate.

This sharpens our eye for the artistic potential of cinema in general. The quality of films is tied not so much to the lofty or banal material with which they engage, but rather primarily to the magnetism of the forms with which they give shape to that material. When this succeeds, so does the artistic object. The quality of a film, whether it follows the mainstream of a particular genre or era or is aimed against it, always depends on the harmony, finesse, and calculation of its timing and its framing. It would be ludicrous to believe that in the cinema, of all places, we would be unable to attend or disallowed from attending to these factors the moment we are ready to succumb to cinema's sensations.

9

FILM AS PHILOSOPHY

Flashbacks

Films like John Ford's *The Searchers* or *The Man Who Shot Liberty Valance* tell stories of the violent establishment of a state of law in a pacified community and society, where the violence of this process still reverberates through the relatively civilized status quo.[1] Among the themes of Alfred Hitchcock's *North by Northwest*, in Stanley Cavell's interpretation, is the theatricality of everyday life and along with it the uncanniness of the ordinary, which one has to accept in order not to lose one's sanity in the face of ordinary life.[2] Michelangelo Antonioni's *Zabriskie Point* contraposes the pseudorevolutionary desire to bring fantasy to power with the power of its own filmic fantasies. *The Bourne Supremacy* by Paul Greengrass, with all the pleasure it takes in its own action-packed drama, is also a film about the depths of personal identity. Antonioni's *Blow-Up* is not only a treatise on the relations between photography and film; at the same time, it tells of its hero's narcissistic fixation on clinging to the moments of his life. At the end of *A Night at the Opera*, in Theodor W. Adorno's words, we see the Marx Brothers "demolish an opera set as if to clothe in allegory the insight of the philosophy of history on the decay of the operatic form."[3] *In the Mood for Love* by Wong Kar-Wai paints the picture of an erotic passion that keeps faith with its own desire by renouncing its consummation. Martin Scorsese's film *Goodfellas* is about the glamour and the misery of a life lived in the state of exception of a criminal internal morality. Francis Ford Coppola's *Apocalypse Now* dramatizes the inability of American participants in the Vietnam War to look reality in the face except through delusional projections. Some commentators on Michael Haneke's film *Caché* have been tempted to interpret the extraterritorial views that drive its narrative in theological or moral-psychological fashion as a God's-eye view or a perspective of conscience. Yet these are futile attempts to explain something for which the film simply offers no explanation. More to the point, the images with which it operates, which remain mysterious, represent a reflection on form embedded in the narrated story. This proposes an ethics of the spectatorial gaze that demands of the audience that it distance itself from the conventions of its own conception of the world.

Another Affair

And so on. In almost every film described or mentioned in this book, and in almost every other film that is even halfway artfully made, it is possible, with a little flair, to discover philosophical substance. It is everywhere present in films where they touch on basic dimensions of human beings' self-awareness and exploration of the world. It is not without reason that Hegel ranked art together with philosophy and religion among the highest forms through which human self-awareness is achieved, though he ties this to a questionable notion of the higher status of philosophy vis-à-vis the arts. To be sure, philosophical analysis of understandings and concepts, without which thinking and acting are impossible—or nearly impossible—typically takes place in a discursive mode; yet from Plato to Wittgenstein, there have been experiments time and again with literary forms of representation as well. There is no fundamental divide between philosophy and the arts.

A key difference between these two genres of human artistry remains in place, however. It lies in our manner of interacting with the works in question. To understand a philosophical concept means to be able to rephrase it in one's own words; a philosophical work—or a work that we treat *as* philosophical—calls out for translation into another language. To understand something as an artistic object, on the other hand, means to be confronted with its individual composition without the expectation of being able to substitute something for it in some way. (The process of translating literary works demands that they be created anew in another language.) The interpretive phrases that we express about an artwork exist, first of all, in order to allow this work to come into appearing in the most intense way possible. The more informative these phrases are, the more they enrich the aesthetic experience of the work.

To attribute philosophical substance to a film does not, by a long stretch, turn the latter into a piece of philosophy. Something analogous is true for the other arts as well. Novels, dramas, images, sculptures, installations, and even buildings or pieces of instrumental music can have philosophical substance and be self-reflexive to the point of excess without for that reason being covert philosophical treatises. Film is no exception here. As in the case of our comparisons with architecture, music, and theater, the "as" in the title of this chapter does not aim to erase the boundaries between philosophy and film. It merely indicates that filmic exploration of human circumstances in the world is related to their philosophical explication. Film shares this relationship with the rest of the arts. It is in the nature of all the arts to carry on affairs, not only with each other, but with philosophy as well.

Three Dimensions

How film touches philosophy, without becoming its equivalent, becomes apparent when we consider the double meaning in the reference to a "philosophy of film." The phrase can be understood in the sense of either a *genitivus objectivus* or a *genitivus subjectivus*. In the first sense, film is placed in the position of an *object* of philosophical aesthetics, which has things to say *about* film's basic operations. In the second sense, film itself is presented as the philosophizing *subject*, as a form of art that shows, in its fundamental operations, a particular affinity—compared to other arts—for philosophy. Throughout this book, I speak *about* film, just as other theories do. Film is the object of my observations, which are devoted to the aesthetic potential of feature films in the cinema. Included in this potential, however, is the fact that film *itself*, by virtue of its basic structure, operates philosophically.

This philosophical temperament of film evinces multiple dimensions. The first two have already been addressed in the initial examples. First, in the mode of exemplary narratives, films can deal with or touch on nearly any topic in philosophy, from ethics to legal, social, and political philosophy, from the philosophy of history, culture, and art to the philosophy of mind and epistemology. Second, in the manner of their composition, they can expose and reflect on their own operation or that of films in general; by virtue of their own forms, they contain elements of a theory of cinema. In films like *The Searchers, North by Northwest, Blow-Up, Caché*, and many others, these two dimensions are frequently at work simultaneously. The third dimension, however, is tied directly to films' sonic and visual dynamics. The basic possibilities of human action and inaction, thought and desire, disposition and sensation, are reflected in it. Successful films offer a new interpretation of film's possibilities and at the same time a new interpretation of actual and potential relations of individual, social, cultural, or political life. In their composition in sound and image, these films alter the spectrum of both their medium and their audience's encounter with the world.

Cine-anthropology

All arts, in their own ways, perform an experiment with the human being's status within the natural and historical world. In the presence of their works, they open up a space, released from the obligations of normal practice, for encountering the self and encountering the world. The status of a particular art form with regard to the other arts derives not least from how it undertakes this. Art's status with regard to philosophy also hinges on the way that each side brings to light the human relationship to the world. Their shared point of reference is in an investigation, from the inside out, of the human form of life. From perspectives of participating in and being ensnared by the human form of life, art and philosophy afford human beings opportunities for, as Heidegger puts it, an "outlook on themselves."[4] In this regard, the arts have always interacted and cooperated with the reflexive enlightenment of philosophy. For the same reason, however, they are in continual conflict with it at the same time. After all, art's nonconceptual exercises bring into appearing the individuality of the real and its experience, which in the discourse of philosophy must remain underdetermined, if it is not ignored entirely. The imagination of cinema also moves within the field of this competition. Its anthropological expeditions lead down paths where philosophical thought cannot follow.[5]

In contrast to the undisturbed nature of an unmoved mover, human life has frequently been viewed as existing in an irresolvable tension between opposing poles—as a perpetual fluctuation between movement and stasis, stress and relaxation; as a pendulum swing between pain and boredom; as an antagonism between the pleasure principle and the death drive. However one may judge any one of these interpretations, together they speak in favor of seeing in the polarity of moving and being-moved a fundamental law of human life—and not only human life. This polarity should be understood, however, neither as a conflict between independent forces nor even primarily as a conflict between opposing ones. It denotes instead a fundamental tension that shapes more active and more passive behavior *equally*. Being-moved and moving work in tandem. We cannot move without being moved; that by which we are moved influences how we move. In everything we strive for, whether bodily or spiritually, we are moved in body and in spirit; everything that moves us physically or psychically modifies our capability for bodily or intellectual movement. This describes not only a situation in which we inevitably find ourselves, but likewise one that we inevitably yearn for in every inclination of our thoughts. We cannot help but to want to be moved, one way or another. We pursue situations that we expect or hope will move us in congenial, surprising, provocative, or otherwise rousing ways. Wherever we exercise self-determination, we also determine to let ourselves be determined.[6]

Film intervenes in this structure of movement and being-moved. The situation in the cinema lends a particular twist to the human being's position between being-determined and determining.[7] Films do not alter the human situation on their own, however; they demonstrate varieties and variations on human being-in-the-world. This is not something they do once and for all, but rather over and over again—and differently each time. "Cine-anthropology"—just the sound of the expression says it all: films play with the possibilities and impossibilities of human experience and expectation by playing through particular constellations of their interrelationship. This book's investigations have been devoted to the form of this imagination. In a different way than the other arts, and yet in a relationship—be it latent or open—with them, the cinematic film organizes its own relations of time and space, image and sound, protention and retention, appearing and disappearing, presence and absence, reference to the world and distance from it, narration and reflection, motion and emotion. Film produces a form of tension between phenomenal movement and the commotion of body and soul in a way that is not found in the other arts.

This became evident even in the first two chapters. The space-time of the cinema opens up a landscape in which every inside corresponds to an outside, and every outside to an inside. In this landscape is fulfilled the divided yearning for spaces of security and, simultaneously, for their transgression. A film like *The Searchers* is concerned from start to finish with this heterogeneous disposition of its characters and of its own medium as well. In *Zabriskie Point* the desert is staged as a space outside of societal constraints. In *Caché*, an external perception insinuates itself disturbingly into the self-perception of the main character and at the same time into the reliability of the filmic perspectives. *In the Mood for Love* lingers almost exclusively in interior spaces, since its protagonists do not permit their passion to break out. These filmic spaces—accessible and inaccessible, opening and closing—occur in a film together with the film's own time. Everything that happens in the course of a film refers to what, in the film, is no longer, not yet, or not at all in the present; in the manner in which it unfolds, the film preserves, in everything, the experience of a vanishing present. The end of *The Searchers* takes up the film's own beginning again in reverse orientation; it releases Ethan Edwards into a future that is just as indeterminate as the prehistory from which he emerged. *Apocalypse Now* begins and ends with the agony of its hero; with that the film repeats a movement that must have already taken place, before its narrative even begins, thus further underscoring the traumatic nature of the main character's experience.

Every film, however, has a different way of disposing its own time and its own space. In the direction its story takes, in the interplay of the perspectives out of which the story unfolds, and in the way the film combines narration and attraction, as well, every individual film attains its individual form and its individual content. The methods of film are thus always different from those of philosophy. Film's aesthetic anthropology proceeds historically and experimentally. Nothing is held fast, once and for all, in a conceptual abstraction. Everything is developed in a bringing into presence of particular situations. Film's explorations always take place in the mode of an exemplary presentation. Through its dispositions, film continually illuminates new facets of the human disposition. The "promise of film," formulated in connection with my interpretation of *Blow-Up*, should also be understood in this way: as a promise to expose the covert within the open, transience within time, happenstance within action, ignorance within knowledge, being-moved within movement. It is a promise that makes understandable why film's countless affairs touch on our own in such manifold respects.

Active Passivity

Something similar is true, as well, for many other art forms and the way they interact with the rest of the arts. In order to recognize, still more precisely, the particular accent that film brings to the arts' flair for the philosophical, we must recall an impulse that film shares with many other arts. Inspiring works in almost every genre of art offer whatever they present in a form that impels their readers, viewers, or listeners to adopt a sensate mode of apprehending, one that is captivating and liberating in the same breath. In a way that other forms of thinking cannot, these works trigger in their perceivers an invigoration of their receptivity and spontaneity, an activation of their susceptibility and sensitivity, which are coupled with their imaginative and cognitive faculties.

In his lectures on aesthetics in the winter semester of 1958/59, Adorno described this rather emphatically, taking music as the example:

> [I]f you truly listen to a complex symphonic movement in such a way that
> you genuinely relate all its sensual aspects to one another, that you hear and

sensually perceive them in their unity and their mediatedness, if you thus hear what you hear not simply in the way it appears to you now but also in its relation to what has already passed in the work and to what still lies ahead of you in the work, and finally to the whole, then this is surely the highest degree of precise sensual experience that can be achieved.[8]

This highly sensuous perception implies at the same time, however, a largely intellectual capacity for comprehension, since one has to follow the web of references in which every passage of the respective work is situated. Adorno warns against understanding the vitality of experiencing powerful artworks in terms of a model of self-assured consumption. "So I would say that aesthetic experience essentially consists in taking part in this co-enactment, in joining the process of the work of art by being inside it, by—to put it very simply—living in it."[9] In this passage, the metaphor of "living" signals, above all, the fact that—and the extent to which—the subject of art's perception is moved by what he or she perceives: "[I]t is less a matter of what the work 'gives' us than what we give to it. That is, whether, in a particular form of active passivity or effortful surrender to the matter, we give it what it actually expects of us."[10]

"Active passivity"—that is crucial term here. The encounter with works of art demands the capacity and the willingness to turn one's attention to them in such a way that their processuality can unfold, indeed, in such a way that the listeners, viewers, or readers are taken along by this process. They *actively* determine to submit to a *passive* being-determined. Whether this takes place, as Adorno puts it, in the mode of an "effortful" involvement, a relaxed participation, or in a fluctuation between the two is nearly inconsequential. Either way, what matters is that one readily surrender to the play of forces of the respective objects. The "precise sensual experience" of art implies a form of attention that remembers and anticipates, differentiates and combines—and thus always interprets.

The image of aesthetic perception that Adorno proposes is one of eager abandon. "These moments are probably the highest and the most decisive . . . for these moments truly have a form of delight to them that—I will not say outshines, but definitely matches the highest moments of happiness one experiences elsewhere; they have the same power as the highest real moments that we know."[11] The term "power" in this passage points, again, to the moment of immersion enabled by one's own

participation. As in the rest of life, so too in our encounter with powerful art objects: we cannot "make" our happiness by our own device, but
rather must acquiesce to it.

An Encore

The particular impetus through which cinema enriches the play of the arts
and other human play is now within reach. In the cinema, we can enjoy
the passive side of our existence in an exceptional way. We can succumb
to a world by letting ourselves and the world be. We are stimulated to a
form of being-moved that also forms the basis of our capacity for action
in other spheres.

But that is not all. Film creates for its viewers, at the same time, a situation in which, by being *outside* of themselves in a certain way, they are
possessed of themselves in a way that other forms of perception, image
perception included, do not allow. By submitting to its visual and acoustic
dictate, spectators come closer than in any other setting to a fulfillment
of their desire for once not to have to determine their position, but rather
to be able to *let* themselves be determined by it. Film provides them with
the particular delights of passivity (and thus sometimes also its torments).
In the space of the cinema, they have the opportunity to let themselves be
touched, emotionally and intellectually, by anything capable of moving
them. Cinematic films can take the configurations of our impulses, affects,
and affinities, in all their opaque mixtures and linkages, and, using convictions and emotions of all sorts, disturb them, unsettle them, play them
through, and in so doing interrogate them in a particular way. We can linger with their movement without danger of being captured by this movement, except in the mode of sensate apprehending and understanding.

Being taken along in this way does not simply arise on its own, however. The cinema, after all, is not a dormitory in which we merely indulge
in our own dreams (although this can sometimes have its charms). It does
demand considerable wakefulness, presence of mind, and attention. Following the imagination of films is always an active effort; in order to go
along with a film, one has to keep up with it. Yet all the activity of understanding, which the perception of art objects always demands, is founded
here, in the cinema, on a heightened passivity. It is heightened with respect

to the passivity that is characteristic of other perception because, in the case of cinema, control over the time and the direction in which it is apprehended is removed from the perceiver to an even greater degree than is otherwise the case in the arts. To have this control removed can be experienced as liberation, however: through an involuntary activation of the passions that grip us or that could grip us. Films afford us an excellent opportunity to live out our heterogeneous dispositions.

The particular ritual to which the cinema invites its visitors is situated in this relatively extreme activation of the receptivity and responsiveness of the cinematic audience. Yet this amounts to nothing more than an encore to the play of forces of the rest of the arts. The give-and-take among the arts is much too intensive for any one of them to lay exclusive claim to any form of presentation. The liberal collective made up of the many arts leaves the individuality of each art form the room-for-play that it needs to thrive, from which, in turn, the others can profit. In the same way, the collective of a single art form grants its individual objects the freedom to realize their rights as citizens, each according to its own fashion. A philosophy of the arts should, in any case, respect this egalitarian state of law, even if the state of affairs is often quite different in practice. Privileges are conferred, hierarchies established, and distribution channels created that are detrimental to free exchange among the arts.

Landscapes, Once Again

This does not mean, however, that the various arts have no privileges vis-à-vis other forms of encountering the world and coming to self-awareness. They have something of an advantage over philosophy, for one, although the latter is not terribly worse off. Presenting the particularity of affairs, they can show what philosophy can only speak about in general terms. This is also the situation as regards philosophy and film. Philosophy can only speak *about* the world: about how we find ourselves and how we feel, essentially, in the world. The feature film, by contrast, can let *its world* speak and in so doing can continually capture new facets of our world. Film lets its world "speak" by engendering and presenting an occurring space through which its present attains the character of a landscape, as described in the first chapter. The dynamics of filmic space and filmic time open up for the audience a

zone of apprehending and understanding within a horizon that simultaneously exceeds understanding and apprehending—as is the case in life situations outside of the cinema as well. Feature films are artificial landscapes
that we explore in sensate observation. By presenting their world in such a
way that they withhold from the spectators much that is in it, they model
for them what it means to inhabit, for a while, a natural, cultural, social,
and historical world.

Then again, these are admittedly only the general assertions of a phi-
losopher. Cinema itself does not stand still for such aphorisms. Each of its
films unfolds its own landscape. Each one explores another side of real or
potential existence amid a present that is, on the whole, opaque. The best
films achieve this in continually different and continually new ways. They
give their time travels an individual form. That is the way films show us
where we stand with ourselves.

CLOSING CREDITS

Notice

In significant parts, this book is the outcome of a collaboration with Angela Keppler. For some time now, our conversations have come, again and again, to revolve around film, television, and many related topics. In the process, we have turned over certain thoughts together and pushed certain concepts back and forth across our real and virtual desktops so often that, by now, we can only view them as shared assets. Of course, we each take sole responsibility for our own writing in our respective publications; any errors or missteps contained in this book are mine and mine alone.

Thanks

I have presented fragments and versions of this book in many settings since 2005 and have greatly profited from the suggestions and critique offered by many people. Among them are Thomas Assheuer, Andrew Benjamin, Georg Bertram, Noël Carroll, James Conant, Lorenz Engell, Astrid Erll, Oliver Fahle, Daniel Feige, Alessandro Ferrara, Josef Früchtl, Lydia Goehr, Helena Grass, Tonino Griffero, Norbert Grob, Tom Gunning, Michael Hampe, Vinzenz Hediger, Jochen Hörisch, Renate Hörisch, Bernd Kiefer, Gertrud Koch, Morten Kyndrup, Christopher Latiolais, Jasper Liptow, Arne Melberg, Henrik Oxvig, Carlos Pereda, Robert Pippin, Regine Prange, Juliane Rebentisch, Birgit Recki, Christian Refsum, Sebastian Rödl, Eivind Røssaak, Marcela Rodríguez, Wilmar Sauter, Ludger Schwarte, Benjamin Seel, Achim Vesper, Christiane Voss, Thomas Wartenberg, Lambert Wiesing, George Wilson, and Hans Jürgen Wulff. I would like to express my sincere thanks to them all.

I also owe a debt of gratitude to the students in Frankfurt and Vienna who, in my lectures on the motifs of this book, insistently challenged me on all the right points.

"The Formation of Normative Orders," the research partnership—or "Cluster of Excellence," as it is known—at the Johann Wolfgang Goethe University of Frankfurt, provided a context for my work that proved productive in many respects.

Eva Backhaus, Stefan Deines, Sebastian Esch, Frederike Popp, and Jochen Schuff guided the book with verve through its final stages, offering critical commentary and uncompromising corrections that averted significant problems.

Alexander Roesler of S. Fischer Verlag kept his nerve, even at the end, and when there was nothing to be done, he stoically let things run their course—just as in the cinema.

Last but not least, I would like to thank Kizer S. Walker for his splendid translation of this book—as well as Marian Rogers for her work copyediting the manuscript and Mahinder Kingra and his colleagues at Cornell University Press for their support of the English edition.

Translator's Note

In working with Martin Seel's elegant text, I have attempted, wherever possible, to convey the style and tone of the original. Admittedly, I have sometimes had to sacrifice elegance to faithfulness to concepts. As regards certain terms that are key for Seel's oeuvre, I have mostly endeavored to keep the text consistent with extant translations of his work into English, in particular John Farrell's masterful rendering of Seel's 2000 *Ästhetik des Erscheinens* (published by Stanford University Press in 2005 as *Aesthetics of Appearing*). Naturally, though, concepts and emphases specific to the present work have suggested directions that sometimes diverge from previous translations.

The Arts of Cinema deals throughout with questions surrounding degrees of agency and passive receptivity in the perception of films and other artworks. Some of the most important distinctions the book makes in this regard have been the most challenging to capture in translation. One key distinction is that between perception mediated by cognition (*Wahrnehmung*) and a more immediate taking-in of visual and sonic stimuli by the senses (*Vernehmen*). I have translated the latter in most instances as "apprehending." Another is the distinction between *moving* and *being-moved*. Many of the constructions having to do with moving (*bewegen*) that recur in the book are built on the past participle form (*bewegt*), which can denote the passive voice in some contexts. In German, as in English, "being moved" can refer to a change of position or to a state of being stirred emotionally. This double sense is stronger and closer to the surface in German, however, which presents a particular challenge for capturing the full nuance in some of Seel's passages; there are, no doubt, instances in the book where that nuance is partly lost. *Bewegtsein* is rendered throughout the book as "being-moved." I have translated the related term *Bewegtheit* simply as "motion" in most cases, other times as "emotion" and even psychic "commotion," depending on context. In a book concerned so centrally with moving images—*Bewegtbilder*—and the role of spectators' emotions in their (passive and active) reception in the cinema, this cluster of meaning is usually close at hand.

In most cases, I have been able to draw on extant English versions of texts cited in German by Seel in the original; wherever a published English edition is available, the reference is only to the English. Where there was no extant English version of a text cited in German by Seel, I have supplied the English translation.

I would like to express my sincere thanks to Martin Seel and Peter Gilgen for their advice and suggestions during certain stages of the translation process. Any remaining infelicities or lack of clarity is my responsibility alone.

—Kizer S. Walker

NOTES

Opening Credits

1. *Translator's note:* Miriam Hansen proposes this literal translation of *Spielraum* in Walter Benjamin's usage with regard to the open-ended, imaginative qualities of film. Hansen, *Cinema and Experience: Siegfried Kracauer, Walter Benjamin, and Theodor W. Adorno* (Berkeley: University of California Press, 2012). I use "room-for-play" for *Spielraum* throughout this book.

1. Film as Architecture

1. Georg Wilhelm Friedrich Hegel, *Aesthetics: Lectures on Fine Art*, trans. T.M. Knox (Oxford: Clarendon, 1975), 2:894.

2. *Translator's note:* The German terms here are "Geräusch" and "Klang," respectively, which do not align perfectly with the English terms I have chosen here. *Geräusch* is related to the English "rush" and has its origins in an imitative description of the sound of moving water or wind. In the context of cinema, the term may describe ambient sounds—mechanical noises, sounds of nature, voices heard in the background of a film, and so on. The term *Klang* can connote a pleasing or harmonious sound, such as the ringing of bells or the timbre of the human voice. Like the English "tone," it can describe a sound with reference to its acoustic qualities, but the term is also used to denote sound more generally. Crucially, here, it can connote the depth dimension of acoustic phenomena, the resonance of sound in three-dimensional space. Neither "resonance" nor "tone" captures the sense of *Klang* in all cases,

and I have variously used "sound" or other near synonyms elsewhere in the book, depending on context. In this book, *Klang* often appears in the compound adjective *klangbildlich*, a key construction for Martin Seel's theory of cinema that I have translated as "sonic and visual" in most instances. It is worth noting here that another acoustic term—*Ton*—is the standard German for "sound" in the sense of film's audio dimension (the German term for "sound film" is *Tonfilm*).

3. *Translator's note:* Seel refers here to "eines spürenden Vernehmens." The verb *spüren* means "sensing" or "feeling"; the verb *vernehmen* (used in its noun form here) usually refers to acoustic perception—taking in information about the world by the sense of hearing—but it can denote a "taking in" more generally. Seel is concerned with the continuum, in aesthetic experience, from sensation to taking in or apprehending a sensation to cognitive processes of perceiving or understanding what has been taken in.

4. Filmic movement only comes about, according to Gilles Deleuze, "if the whole is neither given nor giveable." Deleuze, *Cinema*, trans. Hugh Tomlinson and Barbara Habberjam, vol. 2, *The Movement-Image* (Minneapolis: University of Minnesota Press, 1986), 7.

2. Film as Music

1. On the position of music among the arts, see Albrecht Wellmer, *Versuch über Musik und Sprache* (Munich: Hanser, 2009), esp. chap. 2.

2. Angela Keppler, *Mediale Gegenwart: Eine Theorie des Fernsehens am Beispiel der Darstellung von Gewalt* (Frankfurt: Suhrkamp, 2006), 66.

3. Hegel, *Aesthetics*, 1:891.

4. *Translator's note:* "Großrhythmus." Miriam Hansen renders the usage in Adorno and Eisler's *Komposition für den Film* as "higher rhythm." See Hansen, *Cinema and Experience*, 246. While the German manuscript was completed in 1944, the Adorno and Eisler text was first published in English, appearing with Oxford University Press in 1947 under the title *Composing for the Films*. An abridged German edition followed in 1949; the first full edition appeared in German in 1969. Adorno and Eisler defined *Großrhythmus*, without offering an English equivalent, as "the proportion between the parts and their dynamic relationship, the progression or the stopping of the whole, the breath pattern, so to speak, of the total form." Theodor Adorno and Hanns Eisler, *Composing for the Films* (London and Atlantic Highlands, NJ: Athlone Press, 1994), 68.

5. Adorno and Eisler, *Composing for the Films*, 70.

3. Film as Image

1. Richard Wollheim, "Seeing-as, Seeing-in, and Pictorial Representation," in *Art and Its Objects: With Six Supplementary Essays*, 2nd ed. (Cambridge: Cambridge University Press, 1980), 137–151; Gottfried Boehm, "Die Wiederkehr der Bilder," in *Was ist ein Bild?* ed. Gottfried Boehm (Munich: Fink, 1994), 11–38. Cf. Boehm, "Die Bilderfrage," in *Was ist ein Bild?*, 325–343. Cf., in the same volume, Michael Polanyi, "Was ist ein Bild?," 148–162. Also Martin Seel, "Dreizehn Sätze über das Bild," in *Ästhetik des Erscheinens* (Munich: Hanser, 2000), 255–293.

2. Max Imdahl, *Giotto. Arenafresken. Ikonographie—Ikonologie—Ikonik* (Munich: Fink, 1980), esp. 26 and 84; cf. Imdahl, "Ikonik: Bilder und ihre Anschauung," in *Was ist ein Bild?* ed. Boehm, 300–324.

3. André Bazin, *What Is Cinema?* trans. Hugh Gray (Berkeley: University of California Press, 1967), 1:105.

4. Stanley Cavell, *The World Viewed: Reflections on the Ontology of Film*, Harvard Film Studies (Cambridge, MA: Harvard University Press, 1979), 24.

5. *Translator's note:* The German term here is "Anschein."

6. A counterargument is advanced in the following: Kendall L. Walton, "Transparent Pictures: On the Nature of Photographic Realism," in *Marvelous Images: On Values and the Arts* (Oxford: Oxford University Press, 2008), 79–116; Dominic McIver Lopes, "The Aesthetics of Photographic Transparency," in *Philosophy of Film and Motion Pictures: An Anthology*, ed. Noël Carroll and Jinhee Choi (Malden, MA: Blackwell, 2006), 35–43.

7. Martin Seel, "The Imagination of Photography," in *Konzept: Fotografie REAL*, ed. Luminita Sabau (Ostfildern: Hatje Cantz, 2008), 20–33.

8. Roland Barthes once reflected in passing on the aptness of "the view that the distinction between film and photograph is not a simple difference of degree but a radical opposition. Film can no longer be seen as animated photographs: the having-been-there gives way before a being-there of the thing." Roland Barthes, "Rhetoric of the Image," in *Image, Music, Text*, ed. and trans. Stephen Heath (New York: Hill and Wang, 1977), 32–51; 45.

4. Film as Spectacle

1. Erwin Panofsky, "Style and Medium in the Motion Pictures," in *Three Essays on Style*, ed. Irving Lavin (Cambridge, MA: MIT Press, 1995), 91–128; 96.

2. Panofsky, "Style and Medium," 96–98; cf. André Bazin, "Theatre and Cinema," in *What Is Cinema?* 1:76–124; also Cavell, *The World Viewed*, 26–29.

3. This alone is enough to shatter the stubborn prejudice that claims there is no film-specific construction of space in the traditional animated film. "Cartoons are not movies" is the verdict of Cavell (*The World Viewed*, 168).

4. Here I am in agreement with Cavell, *The World Viewed*, 27ff.

5. Cf. Keppler, *Mediale Gegenwart*, 309–310.

6. Tom Gunning, "An Aesthetic of Astonishment: Early Film and the (In)Credulous Spectator," in *Viewing Positions: Ways of Seeing Film*, ed. Linda Williams (New Brunswick, NJ: Rutgers University Press, 1994), 114–133; 121.

7. Gunning provides only sparse indications pertaining to this. Cf. Tom Gunning, "The Cinema of Attraction(s): Early Film, Its Spectator, and the Avant-Garde," in *Early Cinema: Space, Frame, Narrative*, ed. Thomas Elsaesser (London: BFI, 1990), 56–62.

5. Film as Narrative

1. Wolfgang Iser, *The Act of Reading: A Theory of Aesthetic Response* (Baltimore: Johns Hopkins University Press, 1978).

2. Michael Hampe, *Kleine Geschichte des Naturgesetzbegriffs* (Frankfurt: Suhrkamp, 2007), 26 (emphasis in the original).

3. Peter Goldie, *The Mess Inside: Narrative, Emotion, and the Mind* (Oxford: Oxford University Press, 2012), 13.

4. Goldie, *The Mess Inside*, 32.

5. Goldie, *The Mess Inside*, 32.

6. For a contrary position, see, e.g., Cavell, *The World Viewed*, 26; Dudley Andrew, *What Cinema Is! Bazin's Quest and Its Charge* (Chichester: Wiley-Blackwell, 2010), 87–88.

7. Arthur C. Danto, *Narration and Knowledge* (New York: Columbia University Press, 2007), 342–383; 343.

8. Danto, *Narration and Knowledge*, 353; cf. 363.

9. Like all documentary forms of cinema, live broadcasts exploit the photographic potential of film in a particular way—more on this in the next chapter.

10. Cf. Martin Seel, *Aesthetics of Appearing*, trans. John Farrell (Stanford, CA: Stanford University Press, 2005), esp. 105–138.

6. Film as Exploration

1. Keppler, *Mediale Gegenwart*, 179.

2. Keppler, *Mediale Gegenwart*, 180; cf. 158–184 (emphasis in the original).

3. James Conant, "The World of a Movie," in *Making a Difference: Rethinking Humanism and the Humanities*, ed. Niklas Forsberg and Susanne Jansson (Stockholm: Thales, 2011), 293–324; 298.

4. Conant, "The World of a Movie" 301.

5. Keppler, *Mediale Gegenwart*, 158–159 and 179–180.

6. See above, chapter 3.

7. Dudley Andrew, *What Cinema Is!* xxv.

8. On this thesis, see Keppler, *Mediale Gegenwart*, 64 and 160; also Martin Seel, "Realism and Anti-Realism in Film Theory," trans. Joseph Ganahl, *Critical Horizons* 9, no. 2 (Sept. 2008): 157–175, esp. 166 and 173ff.; cf. Seel, "Im Zweifelsgewann: Jürgen Wiesners fotographische Passagen zwischen Natur und Kunst," in *Die Macht des Erscheinens: Texte zur Ästhetik* (Frankfurt: Suhrkamp, 2007), 248. Also, Vinzenz Hediger, "Vom Überhandnehmen der Fiktion: Über die ontologische Unbestimmtheit filmischer Darstellung," in *"Es ist als ob": Fiktionalität in Philosophie, Film- und Medienwissenschaft*, ed. Gertrud Koch and Christiane Voss (Munich: Fink, 2009), 163–183.

9. A contrary position is taken, for example, by D. N. Rodowick, *The Virtual Life of Film* (Cambridge, MA: Harvard University Press, 2007).

7. Film as Imagination

1. E.g., Thomas E. Wartenberg, "Ethics or Film Theory? The Real McGuffin in *North by Northwest*," in *Hitchcock and Philosophy: Dial M for Metaphysics*, ed. David Baggett and William A. Drumin (Chicago: Open Court, 2007), 141–155.

2. George M. Wilson, *Narration in Light: Studies in Cinematic Point of View* (Baltimore: Johns Hopkins University Press, 1986), 64.

3. Wilson, *Narration in Light*, 78.

4. Wilson, *Narration in Light*, 78.

5. Illusionistic argumentation, in a narrower or broader sense, or at least trace elements of illusionism, can be found in, e.g., Albert Michotte, "The Character of 'Reality' of Cinematographic Projection," trans. A. P. Costall, in *Michotte's Experimental Phenomenology of Perception*, ed. Georges Thinès, Alan Costall, and George Butterworth (Hillsdale, NJ: Erlbaum, 1991), 197–209; Christian Metz, "On the Impression of Reality in the Cinema," in *Film Language: A Semiotics of the Cinema*, trans. Michael Taylor (Chicago: University of Chicago Press, 1991), 3–15; Kendall L. Walton, *Mimesis as Make-Believe: On the Foundations of the Representational Arts* (Cambridge, MA: Harvard University Press, 1990); Richard Allen, *Projecting Illusion: Film Spectatorship and the Impression of Reality* (Cambridge: Cambridge University Press, 1995); Colin McGinn, *The Power of Movies: How Screen and Mind Interact* (New York: Pantheon, 2005); George M. Wilson, *Seeing Fictions in Film: The Epistemology of Movies* (Oxford: Oxford University Press, 2011); Christiane Voss, *Der Leihkörper: Erkenntnis und Ästhetik der Illusion* (Munich: Fink, 2013). Arthur C. Danto formulates a general critique of illusionism in the theory of art in *The Transfiguration of the Commonplace: A Philosophy of Art* (Cambridge, MA: Harvard University Press, 1981), chap. 6. For a critique of the variety native to film theory, see Noël Carroll, "Towards an Ontology of the Moving Image," in *Philosophy and Film*, ed. Cynthia A. Freeland and Thomas E. Wartenberg (New York: Routledge, 1995), 68–85; and Seel, "Realism and Anti-Realism."

6. E.g., Vinzenz Hediger, "Wirklichkeitsübertragung: Filmische Illusion als medienhistorische Zäsur bei André Bazin und Albert Michotte," in . . . *kraft der Illusion*, ed. Gertrud Koch and Christiane Voss (Munich: Fink, 2006), 205–230.

7. "In viewing a photograph of a class reunion . . . one actually sees the members of the class, albeit indirectly via the photograph, but at the same time imagines seeing them directly without photographic assistance. In the case of non-documentary films, what we actually see (the actors and the movie set) may be different from what we imagine seeing (the characters, a murder, a chariot race)." Kendall L. Walton, "On Pictures and Photographs: Objections Answered," in *Marvelous Images: On Values and the Arts* (Oxford: Oxford University Press, 2008) 117–132; 127.

8. *Translator's note:* In the original, "eines verstehenden Vernehmens." See note 3 above, in chapter 1, on "sensate apprehending."

9. *Translator's note:* The term is "aufgehoben": "suspended" or "sublated."

10. Siegfried Kracauer, *Theory of Film: The Redemption of Physical Reality* (1960) (Princeton, NJ: Princeton University Press, 1997); André Bazin, "The Ontology of the Photographic Image," in *What Is Cinema?* 9–16.

11. *Translator's note:* The distinction in the German original is between "etwas *Dagewesenes*" and "das *Dasein*" (emphasis in the original).

12. Seel, *Aesthetics of Appearing*, 66–69.

8. Film as Emotion

1. Immanuel Kant, *Anthropology from a Pragmatic Point of View*, trans. and ed. Robert B. Louden, Cambridge Texts in the History of Philosophy (Cambridge: Cambridge University Press, 2006), 127.

2. Kant, *Anthropology*, 127 (emphasis in the original).

3. Cf. Vivian Sobchack, "What My Fingers Knew," in *Carnal Thoughts: Embodiment and Moving Image Culture* (Berkeley: University of California Press, 2004), 53–84. Christiane Voss prefers an illusionistic interpretation of this set of relations. See Voss, *Der Leibkörper*.

4. *Translator's note:* Here, Martin Seel traces a path from apprehending or taking in sensations ("Vernehmen") to their perception ("Wahrnehmung") at a more cognitive level. The concept of "sensate understanding" ("spürendes Verstehen") referred to here highlights the dual quality of aesthetic experience, which, in Seel's view, remains at once a cognitive and a sensuous experience. Cf. notes 3 and 8 above, in chapters 1 and 7, respectively.

5. Cf. Martin Seel, "Was geschieht hier? Beim Verfolgen einer Sequenz in Michelangelo Antonionis Film *Zabriskie Point*," in *Kunst und Erfahrung: Beiträge zu einer philosophischen Kontroverse*, ed. Stefan Deines, Jasper Liptow, and Martin Seel (Berlin: Suhrkamp, 2012), 181–194.

6. On the following, see Martin Seel, "Expressivität: Eine kleine Phänomenologie," in *Expressionismus in den Künsten*, ed. Marion Saxer and Julia Cloot (Hildesheim: Olms, 2012), 25–36.

7. Kant, *Anthropology*, 127.

8. *Translator's note:* The German term here is "Anteilnahme," literally "taking part," which can also be translated as "sympathy" (also in the sense of "condolence").

9. The following studies explore this same line of thinking in greater detail: Murray Smith, *Engaging Characters: Fiction, Emotion, and the Cinema* (Oxford: Clarendon, 1995); Carl Plantinga, *Moving Viewers: American Film and the Spectator's Experience* (Berkeley: University of California Press, 2009); Julian Hanich and Winfried Menninghaus, "Im Wechselbad der Gefühle: Zur Emotionsvielfalt im filmischen Melodram—Eine Mikroanalyse," *Zeitschrift für Ästhetik und Allgemeine Kunstwissenschaft* 56 (2011): 175–201.

10. *Translator's note:* The original here is "Inderweltsein."
11. On the discussion of the status of feelings with regard to fictional characters, cf. Goldie, *The Mess Inside*, 81ff.

9. Film as Philosophy

1. Martin Seel, "Ethan Edwards und einige seiner Verwandten," *Merkur* 63 (2009): 954–964; Seel, *"The Man Who Shot Liberty Valance* oder Von der Undurchsichtigkeit normativen Wandels," in *Formen kulturellen Wandels*, ed. Stefan Deines, Daniel Martin Feige, and Martin Seel (Bielefeld: transcript, 2012), 221–246; Robert B. Pippin, *Hollywood Westerns and American Myth: The Importance of Howard Hawks and John Ford for Political Philosophy* (New Haven, CT: Yale University Press, 2010).
2. Stanley Cavell, "North by Northwest," in *A Hitchcock Reader*, ed. Marshall Deutelbaum and Leland Poague (Chichester: Wiley-Blackwell, 2009), 250–263.
3. Theodor Adorno, "On the Fetish-Character in Music and the Regression of Listening," in *Essays on Music*, ed. Richard Leppert (Berkeley: University of California Press, 2002), 288–317; 314.
4. Martin Heidegger, "The Origin of the Work of Art," in *Off the Beaten Track*, ed. and trans. Julian Young and Kenneth Haynes (Cambridge: Cambridge University Press, 2002), 1–56; 21.
5. Martin Seel, "The Appearance of Spaces in Film," in *Paradoxes of Appearing: Essays on Art, Architecture, and Philosophy*, ed. Michael Asgaard Andersen and Henrik Oxvig (Baden: Lars Müller, 2009), 109–127. Cf. Edgar Morin, *The Cinema, or the Imaginary Man*, trans. Lorraine Mortimer (Minneapolis: University of Minnesota Press, 2005).
6. Martin Seel, "Letting Oneself Be Determined: A Revised Concept of Self-Determination," in *Philosophical Romanticism*, ed. Nikolas Kompridis (London: Routledge, 2006), 81–96.
7. *Translator's note:* The distinction here in the original is between "Bestimmtsein" and "Bestimmendsein."
8. Theodor W. Adorno, *Aesthetics*, ed. Eberhard Ortland, trans. Wieland Hoban (Malden, MA: Polity, 2018), 115.
9. Adorno, *Aesthetics*, 117.
10. Adorno, *Aesthetics*, 118.
11. Adorno, *Aesthetics*, 123.

NAME INDEX

FILM INDEX